Behin
Curt

All about the essence of theater

©Lionel Mazet, 2023

All rights reserved. No part of this book may be reproduced or transmitted in any form or by any means, electronic or mechanical, including photocopying, recording or any information storage system, without the written permission of the author, except for a brief quotation in a review or newspaper article.

Contents

Introduction **6**

Definition of Theatre 6
Objectives and Functions of Theatre 7
Importance and Role of Theatre in Society 8
Different Forms of Theatre 10

The Origins of Theatre **12**

Theatre in Primitive Societies 12
Rituals and Religious Ceremonies 13

Ancient Theatre **17**

Greek Theatre: Evolution of Genres: Tragedy and Comedy 17
Greek Theatre: Major Playwrights: Aeschylus, Sophocles, Euripides, and
Aristophanes 18
Greek Theatre: Places and Specificities of Greek Theatre 20
Roman Theatre: Influence of Greece and Roman Adaptations ... 21
Roman Theatre: Major Playwrights: Plautus, Terence, and Seneca ... 23
Roman Theatre: Places and Specificities of Roman Theatre 24

Medieval Theatre in the Middle Ages **27**

The Early Medieval Theatrical Forms: Mysteries, Miracles, and Morality Plays ... 27
The Birth of Secular Theatre: Farces and Soties 28
The Influence of the Church and the Representation of Religious Life 30
Influences of Arab and Oriental Theatre in the Middle Ages 31

The Theatre in the Renaissance **33**

The Influence of Humanism and Antiquity 33
The Development of Genres during the Renaissance: Tragedy, Comedy, and
Tragicomedy 34
Italian Theatre: Commedia dell'arte 36
Italian Theatre: Intermezzi 38

French Theatre: Humanist Tragedies...39
French Theatre: Humanist Comedies...40
English Theatre: William Shakespeare Life and Works.........................42
English Theatre: Elizabethan Theatre..43
Baroque Theatre in Spain...45

Classical Theater...47

The rules of classical theater 47
Classical Tragedy and Comedy..48
Great Playwrights: Corneille, Molière, and Racine................................50
The Role of Women on Stage...51
French Theater of the 17th Century..53
The Spanish Theater of the Golden Age...55
English Theater of the Restoration 56

Theatre in the 18th and 19th Century 58

Bourgeois Drama 58
Comedy of Manners 60
Melodrama and Vaudeville...61
Great Playwrights: Marivaux, Beaumarchais, and Voltaire....................62
The Birth of Realistic and Naturalistic Theatre......................................64

Modern Theatre (20th Century)..66

The Theatre of the Absurd and Existentialism 66
Major authors: Beckett, Ionesco, and Genet 67
Epic Theatre and Theatre of Engagement...69
Major authors: Brecht, Sartre, and Weiss 70
Theatre of the Intimate and Everyday Life 72
Augusto Boal's Theatre of the Oppressed...73
Innovations in Stage and Theatrical Design in Modern Theatre...........75

Contemporary Theatre 77

Postmodern Theatre 77
Immersive and Interactive Theatre 78

Technical and Aesthetic Aspects of Theatre 81

Genres and Styles 81
Dramatic Structure 82
Stage Space and Set Designs 84
Stage Direction Approach 86
The Art of Interpretation and Acting Techniques 87
Training Schools and Great Actors in History 89
Lighting and Music 90
Evolution of the Audience and Theatres 91
Critics and Awards 93

Theatre Around the World 96

Chinese Theatre 96
Japanese Theatre 97
Indian Theatre 99
African Theatre 100
Latin American Theatre 102

Theatre Professions 106

Actors and Actresses 106
Directors 107
Playwrights and Screenwriters 109
Technicians and Designers 110
Costumers and Makeup Artists 112

Stage Spaces and Scenography 114

The Evolution of Stage Spaces 114
Elements of Scenography 115
Technological Innovations 117
Famous Theaters Around the World 118

Theatre and Other Arts...............121

Music and Opera...............121
Dance and Ballet...............122
Cinema and Visual Arts 123

Theatre and Society...............125

Theatre as a Tool of Power and Propaganda...............125
Theatre and Social and Political Issues...............126
The Role of Theatre in Education and Training...............128
Theatre and Therapy: Theatre as a Tool for Personal Transformation 129

Challenges and Perspectives of Theatre in the 21st Century..... 133

Economic Stakes and the Survival of Theatre Companies 133
Invitation to Reconnect with Theatre in the 21st Century...............135
Acknowledgment...............136

Introduction

Definition of Theatre

The definition of theatre is a complex and subtle question that can vary depending on the times and cultures. However, in its most general form, theatre can be defined as an art of representation that involves the staging of a story, narrative, or situation by actors in front of an audience.

Theatre is a living art that thrives on the physical presence of actors on stage, as well as the active participation of the audience. This art form combines writing, staging, performance, music, dance, scenography, and interaction with the audience. Actors play different roles, using their bodies, voices, gestures, and facial expressions to bring characters to life and tell a story.

Theatre can serve multiple purposes, such as entertaining, educating, critiquing, or moving the audience. It can also be a means of exploring social, political, religious, or psychological issues. Theatre can reflect society and its evolution, as well as stimulate critical thinking and awareness.

Theatre is present in many cultures around the world and can take very different forms depending on local traditions. It can be traditional theatre, such as Japanese Noh or Indonesian shadow theatre, or more contemporary forms, such as absurd theatre or immersive theatre.

Theatre can be considered a demanding art that requires

a high level of skill and collaboration from all participants. Directors, playwrights, actors, technicians, designers, and costume makers work together to create an immersive and memorable theatrical experience for the audience.

In summary, theatre is a rich and complex art that has evolved over the centuries to become a universal and timeless form of expression. It is capable of captivating, educating, entertaining, and provoking the audience, and continues to be an essential tool for communication and reflection in our society.

Objectives and Functions of Theatre

Theatre is an art form that dates back thousands of years and continues to play an important role in our society. The main objective of theatre is to tell a story through live performance in front of an audience. Theatre can have several functions, which vary depending on the times, cultures, and contexts.

In the past, theatre has often been used as a means of conveying important stories and teachings through dramatic performances. Traditional functions of theatre include education, entertainment, reflection, catharsis, contestation, communication, cultural preservation, and artistic expression.

Theatre can be used to educate the audience on important subjects such as politics, history, religion, science, and the arts. Theatre can also be used to entertain the audience and make them reflect on important subjects in a playful and enjoyable way. Theatrical performances can evoke emotions and provide catharsis, which is an emotional release for the spectators. Theatre can also be used as a means of contestation, criticizing and questioning social norms and values.

Theatre is also a means of communication. Theatrical performances can bring together people from different cultures, languages, and perspectives and provide them with a platform to share ideas and experiences. Theatre can also help preserve cultures and local traditions by celebrating them through artistic performances.

Artistic expression is another major objective of theatre. Actors, directors, and playwrights can use theatre to explore and express complex human ideas, emotions, and experiences. Theatre can offer a unique perspective on human life by allowing artists to create stories and characters that reflect the realities of the world we live in.

Importance and Role of Theatre in Society

Theatre is an ancient art that has played an important role in the history of humanity. More than just a form of art, theatre has been and continues to be a tool for communication, expression, and the transmission of important values and messages. It has been used to educate, entertain, inform, criticize, reflect, and engage society.

Theatre has been and continues to be a privileged place for gathering, sharing, and meeting between individuals, communities, and cultures. It has contributed to the creation and maintenance of social bonds, solidarity, and cohesion among human beings. As a place of representation and exchange, theatre has allowed individuals to confront their ideas, beliefs, and opinions, to question social norms and values, and to promote dialogue and debate.

Theatre has also played an important role in the promotion and defense of human rights, democracy, and freedom of expression. By using art to address sensitive and controversial subjects, theatre has raised awareness among citizens about societal issues, denounced injustices and discrimination, promoted equality and diversity, and fostered respect for differences.

Theatre has also been used as a tool for personal transformation and personal development. By allowing individuals to put themselves in the shoes of other characters and experience situations different from their daily lives, theatre has promoted awareness, reflection, and empathy. It has thus contributed to the education of individuals by allowing them to better know themselves, develop their creativity and imagination, and strengthen their self-confidence.

Finally, theatre also has an important economic role. As an artistic and cultural sector, theatre has contributed to job creation, the training of qualified professionals, economic growth, and the cultural influence of countries. It has supported the cultural industry and participated in the promotion of culture and the arts to the general public.

Different Forms of Theatre

Theatre is an art form that has evolved over the centuries and comes in many forms. From classical theatre to experimental theatre, each genre has its own characteristics that set it apart from others. In this section, we will explore the most common forms of theatre.

Firstly, there is classical theatre, which is characterized by a rigid structure, formal dialogues, and elevated language. Classical theatre is divided into two genres: tragedy and comedy. Tragedies portray noble characters facing moral dilemmas, while comedies focus on comical situations and misunderstandings. The great authors of classical theatre include Corneille, Molière, and Racine.

Next, there is modern theatre, which emerged in the early 20th century and is characterized by scenic innovations and more informal dialogues. Absurdist and existentialist theatre, popularized by authors such as Samuel Beckett, Eugène Ionesco, and Jean Genet, is one of the most well-known sub-genres of modern theatre. Epic theatre and theatre of engagement, popularized by Bertolt Brecht, Jean-Paul Sartre, and Peter Weiss, are also important sub-genres.

Contemporary theatre, which emerged in the 1960s and 1970s, is characterized by a wide diversity of styles and forms. Postmodern theatre, which challenges the conventions of traditional theatre, is one of the most well-known sub-genres. New forms of representation, such as immersive and interactive theatre, are also becoming increasingly popular.

Experimental theatre is a form of theatre that focuses on the exploration of new forms and techniques. This form of theatre is often associated with artistic movements such as surrealism and dadaism.

Musical theatre, also known as a musical, is a form of theatre that combines music, singing, and dancing. Musicals are often based on popular literary or film works.

Street theatre is a form of theatre that takes place outdoors and often involves audience participation. Street theatre performances are often interactive and can include music, dance, and acrobatics.

Lastly, there is improvised theatre, which is characterized by spontaneous and unscripted performances. Improvised theatre actors often use audience suggestions to create humorous and absurd scenes.

The Origins of Theatre

Theatre in Primitive Societies

Theatre in primitive societies is a fascinating domain of theatre history that dates back to the origin of humanity. This form of theatre has evolved over time to become one of the most popular and influential art forms in our modern society.

Theatre in primitive societies was considered a means of communicating with the gods and expressing collective emotions. The rituals were often linked to natural cycles, such as seasons, moon phases, and weather events. The characters in these rituals were often gods or spirits of nature, and the actors represented them with masks and costumes.

In many cultures, theatre was also used to transmit knowledge and cultural values. The stories told in the rituals were often myths and legends that described the creation of the world, the history of the community, and moral values. Through their performances, actors provided examples of behavior and attitudes that the community should adopt to be in harmony with nature and the gods.

Rituals were often organized by the elders and shamans of the community, who directed the performances and ensured that they adhered to cultural standards. These rituals were often very important and highly attended events, bringing the entire community together in an atmosphere of celebration, joy, and collective emotion.

The origins of theatre in primitive societies can be traced back to prehistoric times, where people used forms of primitive theatre to celebrate important life events such as weddings, births, and funerals. The earliest traces of theatre can be found in the cave paintings of Lascaux, where scenes of dance and ceremonies are depicted.

Theatre in primitive societies evolved over time, transforming into different forms and genres, depending on cultures and historical periods. The most well-known forms of primitive theatre are dance, singing, storytelling, and dramatic games. These forms of theatre were often linked to religious beliefs and spiritual practices of the communities.

In African cultures, for example, primitive theatre was often related to animistic beliefs, where actors represented spirits of nature and ancestors. In Native American cultures, theatre was often associated with shamanic ceremonies, where actors portrayed spirits of nature and cosmic forces. In Asian cultures, primitive theatre was often linked to religious practices, where actors represented gods and demons.

Rituals and Religious Ceremonies

Rituals and religious ceremonies played a crucial role in the development of theatre in primitive societies. Religious ceremonies were often accompanied by chants, dances, and dramatizations intended to honor gods and ancestors. These theatrical performances laid the foundations of theatre and evolved according to the cultural needs and preferences of different societies.

In African cultures, religious rituals were often organized around a theatrical performance that depicted cosmic events, myths, and legends. Actors often played roles of divine characters or mythical heroes. Dances and songs often accompanied these performances, creating an atmosphere of celebration and communion with the spirits. Elaborate and colorful costumes, makeup, and props brought the characters to life.

In North America, indigenous peoples also used theatre to celebrate their religious beliefs. Religious rituals were often connected to nature, and theatrical representations reflected the deep connection between man and nature. Actors portrayed characters such as animals or spirits of nature, using costumes and masks made of natural materials such as leather, wood, and feathers.

In Asian cultures, religious theatre also played an important role in spreading faith. In China, opera theatres were often used to convey values and moral principles to the masses. The shows often mixed religious elements, such as stories of gods and goddesses, with more secular elements, such as stories of heroes and warriors. Actors often used colorful costumes and elaborate makeup to bring their characters to life.

In Japan, religious theatre took the form of Noh, a style of theatre that emerged in the 14th century and is still practiced today. Noh combines music, dance, and storytelling to tell stories of divine and mythical characters. Actors wear elaborate costumes and masks representing characters such as gods, demons, and ghosts.

In India, religious theatre took the form of classical dance performances, such as Bharatanatyam and Kathakali. These dances were often performed in temples to honor Hindu divinities and tell epic stories of Hinduism. The dances were accompanied by live music and recitations of sacred poetry.

In the Western world, religious theatre developed through the performances of mysteries and miracles in churches during the Middle Ages. These plays told biblical stories and miracles and were often performed by members of the clergy. Over time, these performances evolved to include characters such as angels and saints and were used to teach moral lessons to the faithful. The performances were later adapted to include more secular elements and became farces and moralities.

Overall, rituals and religious ceremonies played an important role in the development of theatre worldwide. Theatrical performances were used to honor gods and ancestors, transmit values and moral principles, and tell epic stories. Costumes, makeup, props, and music all contributed to bringing the characters to life and creating an immersive experience for the audience.

Theatre has continued to evolve over time and adapt to new forms of artistic and cultural expression. However, the origins of theatre in rituals and religious ceremonies remain a key element of its history and development. Religious influences shaped the early forms of theatre and continue to resonate in contemporary performances.

Today, rituals and religious ceremonies continue to inspire new forms of theatre, such as immersive and interactive theatre, which allow the audience to actively participate in the theatrical experience. Religious ceremonies have also influenced the architecture of theatres, with designs inspired by places of worship. Ultimately, rituals and religious ceremonies have contributed to shaping the nature of theatrical art and continue to influence its form and evolution.

Ancient Theatre

Greek Theatre: Evolution of Genres: Tragedy and Comedy

Greek theatre is considered one of the starting points in the history of Western theatre. In fact, the Greeks created two distinct dramatic genres: tragedy and comedy. These genres had a considerable influence on subsequent theatrical forms.

Greek tragedy was regarded as a noble and elevated art form that portrayed dramatic events involving heroic characters facing extreme circumstances. Tragic plays were based on myths or famous historical events, such as the stories of Oedipus or Antigone. The most famous tragic playwrights are Aeschylus, Sophocles, and Euripides, whose plays have been studied and performed worldwide.

Greek tragedy had a specific formal structure known as the dramatic cycle, which included an opening or prologue, an entrance of the chorus called parodos, a series of dramatic episodes, choral songs and dances, a climactic moment, a final exit of the chorus called exodos, and an epilogue. This structure was often used to emphasize the most important aspects of the play and give a tragic dimension to the story. Tragic plays were often performed during religious festivals, and actors wore masks to represent different characters.

On the other hand, Greek comedy was a lighter and more entertaining genre, often used to satirize politicians and public figures. Greek comedies also had a specific formal structure, which included an opening or prologue, a comical interlude called parabasis, comedic episodes, choral songs and dances, and a happy ending. The most famous comedies were written by Aristophanes.

In addition to their importance as distinct dramatic genres, Greek tragedy and comedy had a considerable influence on later theatrical forms. Tragedy inspired dramatic genres such as melodrama, drama, and classical tragedy, while comedy inspired genres such as farce and comedy of manners. The formal structure of Greek tragedy also influenced the structure of French classical tragedy, while Greek comedy inspired Italian Commedia dell'arte.

Therefore, Greek theatre is a source of inspiration for modern theatre and a testimony to the creativity and imagination of artists in antiquity. Furthermore, it is worth noting that Greek theatre was closely tied to the religious and cultural traditions of ancient Greece.

Greek Theatre: Major Playwrights: Aeschylus, Sophocles, Euripides, and Aristophanes

Greek theatre is considered one of the greatest artistic movements of all time. Major playwrights of this period, such as Aeschylus, Sophocles, Euripides, and Aristophanes, had a significant influence on the evolution of theatre throughout the ages.

Aeschylus, often regarded as the father of tragedy, was the first to introduce a second actor in his plays, allowing for greater complexity in the plot. He is also known for his trilogies, including the Oresteia, which won awards at the Dionysia, the most important religious festivals of antiquity. This play tells the story of Orestes seeking revenge by killing his mother for the murder of his father. Aeschylus also introduced the concept of divine justice in his plays, where characters had to face the consequences of their actions.

Sophocles, on the other hand, introduced a third actor, which allowed for greater diversity in interactions between characters. He also emphasized the role of psychology in his plays, creating more complex and nuanced characters. His most famous play, Oedipus Rex, is a perfect example of the use of psychology in Greek theatre. It tells the story of a man who tries to uncover the truth about his past but ends up discovering that he killed his own father and married his mother. Sophocles also created other famous plays, such as Antigone, where the main character defies the city's laws to bury her brother.

Euripides, on the other hand, was known for his subversive tendencies, using marginal characters and controversial situations. His most famous play, Medea, tells the story of a woman who kills her own children to seek revenge on her unfaithful husband. This play was controversial at the time because it questioned the traditional role of women in Greek society. Euripides also wrote other famous plays, such as Iphigenia in Aulis and The Trojan Women, which also addressed controversial themes.

Finally, Aristophanes is best known for his satirical comedies, which ridiculed politics and society of his time. His most famous play, The Birds, tells the story of two men who build a city in the sky and rule over birds. This play uses satire to criticize the politics of ancient Greece and highlight the absurdities of everyday life. Aristophanes also created other famous plays, such as Lysistrata, where Greek women go on a sex strike to end the war.

All these playwrights contributed to the evolution of Greek theatre by introducing new elements such as the second and third actors, the use of psychology, and political satire. They also created plays that have stood the test of time and are still performed and appreciated today. Their contributions were essential in making Greek theatre one of the most important artistic movements in the history of art.

Greek Theatre: Places and Specificities of Greek Theatre

Greek theatre is known to be one of the birthplaces of Western theatre, and the specificities of its performance venues have greatly contributed to this reputation.

Greek performance spaces were mainly located outdoors in places such as hills or natural slopes, where spectators could sit on stone seating called «cavea». It was a collective experience that involved citizens and members of society, reflecting the political values of the city-state.

The cavea was the part of the theatre where spectators sat. It was divided into several sections, each reserved for a group of spectators based on their social status. The most prominent citizens sat in the best seats in the front row, while women, foreigners, and slaves were relegated to lesser seats or even the back of the cavea. This reflected the social hierarchies of ancient Greece, where class differences were very pronounced.

The main performance area was the orchestra, a rectangular platform located in the center of the cavea where the performances took place. This is where actors performed and interacted with the chorus, which consisted of ordinary citizens. The orchestra was also the place where offerings were made to the gods, particularly Dionysus, the god of theatre and celebration.

The skene was a large wall or building located behind the orchestra. It was the central element of the set, often painted to represent the setting of the action. Actors entered and exited the skene, allowing them to disappear and reappear in a dramatic manner. The set design was usually simple, with few props, to allow the audience to focus on the plot and performances.

Plays presented at religious festivals, such as the Dionysia, were often tragedies or comedies that addressed themes such as justice, family, and human relationships. Actors wore elaborate and stylized costumes, often with masks to help distinguish characters. Tragic playwrights such as Aeschylus and Sophocles were often also playwrights, which allowed them to design plays for their own staging.

Roman Theatre: Influence of Greece and Roman

Adaptations

Roman theatre was born out of the influence of ancient Greece, but it also developed independently to create a distinct form of theatre. Romans adapted and adopted many aspects of Greek theatre, but they also developed their own unique style that influenced theatre throughout Europe.

Romans were first exposed to Greek theatre during the conquest of Greece in the 3rd century BC. They were particularly impressed by Greek tragedy and comedy, but they were also influenced by satyr plays and satirical dramas. Romans adapted and translated Greek plays into Latin, thus making Greek theatre accessible to the Roman masses.

Roman adaptations introduced new elements into theatre, such as music, dance, and pantomime, which were combined with spoken dialogue to create a more complete spectacle. Roman theatre also incorporated elements of Roman culture, such as circus games and gladiatorial shows, to create an even more grandiose spectacle experience.

Roman theatre was also distinguished by its performance venues. Unlike Greek theatres, Roman theatres were often built outdoors and could accommodate a larger number of spectators. Roman theatres were often semi-circular in shape, with an elevated stage and seating for spectators in tiered seating around it.

Roman theatre produced many famous authors and plays, such as Plautus, Terence, and Seneca. The plays of Plautus and Terence were often comedies that mocked Roman society and its vices, while Seneca's plays were often tragedies that addressed philosophical and moral themes.

In summary, Roman theatre was influenced by Greek theatre but also developed its own unique style. Roman adaptations introduced new elements such as music, dance, and pantomime, while performance venues were more spacious and could accommodate larger audiences. Roman theatre produced many famous authors and plays that left their mark on theatre history.

Roman Theatre: Major Playwrights: Plautus, Terence, and Seneca

Roman theatre underwent significant evolution influenced by Greece, but it also developed its own identity and characteristics. The major playwrights of Roman theatre were Plautus, Terence, and Seneca, each with their own style and unique contributions to the history of theatre.

Plautus is considered one of the greatest comedians of antiquity, with a production of more than 130 plays. His comedies were often adaptations of Greek works, but he also wrote original plays. Plautus was known for his light humor and casual style, as well as his typical comedic characters, such as cunning servants, young lovers, and grumpy old men. His plays were very popular with the audience and influenced later comedies of the Renaissance and modern theatre.

Terence, on the other hand, wrote more sophisticated comedies with a more elaborate style and serious themes.

He also adapted Greek plays but added his own personal touch by introducing more developed female characters and exploring moral and social issues. Terence was known for his skillful use of dialogue and attention to detail, which made him a highly respected playwright in his time. His plays also influenced later theatre, especially 17th-century French theatre.

Finally, Seneca was a playwright of tragedies, with a production of nine plays. His plays were darker and more pessimistic than Greek plays, perhaps reflecting the concerns of his time. Seneca's characters were often tragic figures facing desperate situations, and he explored themes such as death, violence, and madness. Seneca was also a Stoic philosopher and introduced elements of philosophy into his plays, which influenced later European theatre.

In conclusion, the major playwrights of Roman theatre each contributed in their own way to the history of theatre by introducing new styles, themes, and writing techniques. Their influence is still felt in contemporary theatre, making Plautus, Terence, and Seneca important and indispensable figures in the history of theatre.

Roman Theatre: Places and Specificities of Roman Theatre

Roman theatre was a place of spectacle and entertainment for the Roman population, experiencing significant development from the 2nd century BC until the end of the Roman Empire. Theatre was considered a means to entertain the Roman people, to distract them from everyday life and provide them with a moment of pleasure. Unlike Greek theatre, which was primarily reserved for men, Roman theatre was open to all, including women. In fact, women attended performances in large numbers, and some, such as the famous actress Valeria Messalina, even actively participated in the shows.

Roman theatre was also larger than Greek theatre, with a capacity of up to 20,000 people. It was built outdoors, with a semicircular stage area called «cavea», where spectators sat on stone seating to watch the performances. The seating area was divided into several sections based on the spectators' social class, with the wealthier seated in the lower levels and the less fortunate in the upper levels. The cavea was surrounded by a stage wall called «scaenae frons», which was often richly decorated and represented an architectural backdrop in trompe-l'oeil style.

Theatrical performances in Rome were highly diverse and included plays, pantomimes, acrobatics, and gladiatorial fights. Plays were mainly comedies and farces, while dramas were less frequent. Roman comedies were often satirical and ridiculed the Roman society of the time. Pantomimes were silent theatrical performances where actors expressed emotions and actions through dance and body movements. Acrobatics and gladiatorial fights were also highly popular with the Roman audience and were part of the most appreciated shows.

Specifics of Roman theatre also included the use of special effects such as trapdoors, flying machines, and lighting effects to create dramatic effects. Costumes and sets were also highly elaborate, with complex and detailed designs. Actors wore masks to enhance the expression of emotions and to help identify different characters. Sets were often painted with scenes of everyday life or exotic landscapes to add realism and depth to the performances.

Roman theatre was often used for public events and celebrations, such as circus games, religious festivals, and military triumphs. Theatrical performances were also a means for the wealthy and powerful to showcase their generosity and social status.

Medieval Theatre in the Middle Ages

The Early Medieval Theatrical Forms: Mysteries, Miracles, and Morality Plays

The early medieval theatrical forms reflected the importance of religion in the society of the time. Mysteries, miracles, and morality plays were the three main forms of theatre practiced in the Middle Ages and were often presented during religious festivals or special occasions.

Mysteries were plays based on biblical stories, depicting events such as the Creation, the Nativity, or the Passion of Christ. They were performed by guilds or trade corporations, who competed to present the most spectacular productions. The actors were mainly members of these guilds and were chosen for their technical skills rather than acting talent. The costumes and sets were often elaborate, and the performances were often accompanied by music.

Miracles were plays about miraculous events related to the lives of saints. The actors portrayed saintly characters, and the emphasis was on faith and the miracles attributed to these saints. Miracles were also produced by trade guilds and were often presented during religious festivals. The performances were often staged in public places, such as market squares or main streets, and often involved processions or parades to highlight the solemnity and religious significance.

Morality plays were more allegorical, illustrating concepts such as sin and virtue. The characters were often allegorical figures, such as Reason or Lust, representing ideas rather than real individuals. Morality plays were often performed indoors and often involved characters speaking directly to the audience to convey their moral message.

These early theatrical forms were deeply rooted in religion and morality. They reflected the everyday life of the time and provided a form of religious and moral education to the public. Although these theatrical forms have evolved since that time, they laid the foundations of modern Western theatre and allowed for the expansion and popularity of theatre as a living art form.

Medieval theatre also influenced contemporary theatrical forms, particularly in religious productions such as oratorios and operas. The production and staging techniques used at the time have also influenced modern theatrical productions, including costume creation, lighting, and set design.

The Birth of Secular Theatre: Farces and Soties

In the Middle Ages, secular theatre began to emerge alongside religious performances. Farces and soties were the most popular forms of secular theatre at that time.

Farces were short, comedic plays performed by itinerant troupes called «jongleurs.» They featured stereotypical characters such as peasants, soldiers, or misers. Farces were often improvised and could deal with a wide range of subjects, from everyday life to politics and social issues. They were highly popular throughout Europe in the 14th century.

Soties were also short and comedic plays but were more sophisticated than farces. They were performed by professional actors and featured more complex characters, such as judges or doctors. Soties were often used to criticize society and established institutions, making fun of the nobility, the Church, and political authorities. They were highly popular in 15th-century France.

These forms of secular theatre provided a means for the people to express themselves and be entertained. They were also used to criticize the authorities and religious practices of the time. In fact, farces and soties were often considered subversive and were censored in many places.

Additionally, farces and soties were precursors to the Italian commedia dell'arte, which emerged in the 16th century. Commedia dell'arte was a form of improvised theatre featuring stock characters and comedic plots. It was inspired by farces, soties, and traditional Italian theatre.

Farces and soties also influenced Renaissance theatre in France and England. In France, farces evolved into a form of theatre called «morality plays.» In England, farces inspired the first comedic interludes, which were inserted into more serious plays.

The Influence of the Church and the Representation of Religious Life

In the Middle Ages, the Church played a central role in people's lives, and this influence extended to the realm of theatre. Theatrical performances were often linked to religion and aimed to convey religious and moral messages to the faithful.

The earliest forms of medieval theatre were mysteries, miracles, and morality plays. Mysteries portrayed scenes from the Bible and the lives of saints, while miracles staged miraculous healings or divine interventions. Morality plays featured allegorical characters exemplifying moral values or sins.

These performances were often organized by guilds and religious fraternities, who were responsible for staging and producing the plays. Performances took place in churches and public squares, attracting large audiences.

The Church also influenced the representation of characters on stage. The actors were often members of the clergy, and female roles were played by men since women were not allowed to perform. The costumes were often simple, with clothing representing biblical characters or saints.

Beyond the direct influence of the Church, theatrical representations were also influenced by the religious life of the time. Performances took place during religious festivals and were often used to celebrate important events in the life of the Church. For example, Passion plays were performed during Holy Week, while Christmas mysteries took place during Advent.

Influences of Arab and Oriental Theatre in the Middle Ages

The influence of Arab and Oriental theatre in the Middle Ages marked a crucial period in the history of world theatre. This period spanned from the 6th to the 13th century, a time when Arab and Oriental theatre reached its peak. It was during this period that musical dramatic art forms began to emerge, often based on tales and legends.

Stories were usually transmitted orally and were adapted for the theatre. The plays were often performed by professional actors, musicians, dancers, and singers. Arab and Oriental theatre is characterized by the presence of music and dance, which are closely intertwined with dramatic performances.

Arab and Oriental theatre had a significant influence on the development of world theatre, particularly European theatre. It introduced the use of music and dance in theatrical performances, as well as the idea of staging and directing theatrical performances.

Plays were often organized into scenes with changes of scenery and costumes for different characters. This approach influenced the production and direction of European theatre. Moreover, Arab and Oriental theatre also influenced the themes and motifs of European plays. Themes of courage, love, and betrayal were popular in Arab and Oriental theatre and were adopted in European theatre.

The cultural contribution of Arab and Oriental theatre is highly diverse, as it was influenced by the cultures and traditions of many different countries. For example, Persian theatre was influenced by Iranian culture, and Indian theatre was influenced by Indian culture.

Arab and Oriental theatre also influenced the costumes and sets used in European theatre. Costumes were often colorful and elaborate, adorned with intricate ornaments and patterns. Sets were also elaborate, featuring painted landscapes and decorative elements such as columns, arches, and stone walls.

The Theatre in the Renaissance

The Influence of Humanism and Antiquity

The influence of humanism and antiquity on Renaissance theatre was considerable and shaped the genres and dramatic conventions of this period. Humanism, an intellectual movement of the Renaissance, questioned medieval beliefs and sought to reestablish the importance of the individual and their free will. This new perspective led to a rediscovery of ancient culture, particularly that of Greece and Rome, which significantly influenced the aesthetic and theatrical practices of the time.

Renaissance playwrights sought to imitate the classical forms of Greek and Roman theatre, particularly tragedy and comedy. Artists of the time were captivated by ancient culture, considering the beauty, balance, and harmony of Greek culture as models to follow. Authors adopted the rules of classical theatre, such as the concept of decorum, which demanded conformity to the social and moral standards of the time, and the rule of the three unities, which required consistency in time, place, and action.

Tragedy was the preferred genre of Renaissance playwrights. It was characterized by serious action, complex plots, universal morality, and a tragic ending. Tragedies were often based on historical or mythological events and featured noble and heroic characters facing moral and existential dilemmas. The greatest playwrights of the Renaissance, such as Shakespeare and Marlowe, created masterpieces in this genre.

Comedy, on the other hand, was less formal and more popular than tragedy. It was characterized by light action, simple plots, and a happy ending. Comedies often drew upon everyday life situations and portrayed comical and burlesque characters that were often stereotypical. The Commedia dell'arte, an Italian Renaissance theatre genre that emerged in the 16th century, was an example of popular comedy that influenced Western theatre for centuries. Actors often improvised their dialogue, adding a touch of spontaneity and freshness to the performance.

The influence of antiquity was also evident in costumes and set designs. Artists sought to reproduce the clothing and objects of antiquity, giving productions a grand and spectacular character. Actors often wore masks to express their emotions, a practice derived from ancient Greeks.

The Development of Genres during the Renaissance: Tragedy, Comedy, and Tragicomedy

The Renaissance was a pivotal period in the history of Western theatre, characterized by a rediscovery of ancient traditions and the emergence of new genres. Renaissance playwrights were able to revitalize tragedy and comedy by adding new elements such as music, dance, poetry, and philosophy. This evolution led to the creation of tragicomedy, a genre that combines elements of tragedy and comedy.

Tragedy is a genre that was developed in ancient Greece but experienced a revival during the Renaissance. Renaissance tragedies are characterized by complex plots, complex characters, and intense dramatic situations. The subjects often drawn from history or mythology, but Renaissance playwrights also wrote tragedies that reflected the concerns of their time. Tragedies were used to explore themes such as destiny, power, honor, love, and death.

Comedy, on the other hand, is a lighter and more entertaining genre. Renaissance comedies are characterized by humorous situations, stereotypical characters, and often absurd plots. Comedies were often used to criticize society, particularly the nobility and the court. Renaissance playwrights added new elements to comedy, such as satire, social criticism, and morality.

Tragicomedy, a genre developed during the Renaissance, combines elements of tragedy and comedy. Renaissance tragicomedies are characterized by dramatic situations that are resolved in a happy manner and characters who are both tragic and comic. Tragicomedies were used to explore the ambiguities and contradictions of human nature by portraying characters who were both noble and vulgar, honest and deceitful, joyful and melancholic.

In Italy, the Commedia dell'arte emerged, a popular theatre genre characterized by stereotypical characters and improvisation. Interludes, short comic plays performed between acts of a main play, were also popular in Italy.

In France, theatre experienced significant development with

the humanistic tragedies of Pierre Corneille, which were influenced by antiquity and portrayed noble heroes facing moral dilemmas. The humanistic comedies of Molière were also highly popular, featuring comical characters criticizing social flaws.

In England, William Shakespeare was the most famous playwright of this period. His works, including tragedies, comedies, and histories, explored themes such as love, betrayal, revenge, and politics. Elizabethan theatre was also characterized by great creativity and innovative use of the stage space.

In Spain, Baroque theatre was influenced by religion and politics, with authors such as Lope de Vega and Calderón de la Barca. Spanish theatre was also known for its spectacular costumes and sets.

Beyond Europe, theatre also experienced significant development in other parts of the world. Japanese theatre, for example, was influenced by Noh and Kabuki theatre, with elaborate costumes, masks, and highly stylized stage use.

Italian Theatre: Commedia dell'arte

The Commedia dell'arte, literally meaning «comedy of art» in Italian, is a form of popular Italian theatre that emerged in the 16th century. This theatre form was created and performed by itinerant troupes of costumed and masked actors who traveled throughout Italy and the rest of Europe to entertain people of all social classes.

The Commedia dell'arte was characterized by stereotypical characters such as the old miser, the bumbling servant, the charlatan doctor, the swaggering captain, the beautiful young girl, and many others. These characters were often portrayed in an exaggerated and burlesque manner, with colorful costumes and expressive masks that gave them a distinctive appearance. The actors were often professionals who spent years perfecting their art and technique to bring these characters to life.

Improvisation was a key characteristic of the Commedia dell'arte. Actors used basic scenarios but were encouraged to improvise and add their own personal touch to the characters and situations. This improvisation was supported by expressive body language and dramatic gestures, allowing actors to communicate with the audience without having to speak words.

Masks were also an important feature of the Commedia dell'arte. They were used to represent characters, allowing actors to focus on their physical and gestural performance as well as their voice. Masks also allowed actors to play multiple different roles within a single performance, simply by changing masks to change characters.

The Commedia dell'arte had a major influence on European theatre, particularly on French and English theatre. Italian troupes were invited to perform at the French court, where they had a significant influence on the development of the Comédie-Française. Characters from the Commedia dell'arte also inspired many characters in Shakespeare's plays, such as the jester, the cunning servant, and the beautiful young girl.

The Commedia dell'arte also influenced stagecraft in European theatre by introducing the idea of an open stage with little or no scenery, allowing actors to interact directly with the audience. Actors also began using props such as sticks, swords, and whips to add movement and action to their performances.

Finally, the Commedia dell'arte also had an impact on the development of modern theatrical forms such as vaudeville and burlesque. The themes and characters of the Commedia dell'arte have also been used in other media forms, such as comics, film, and television.

Italian Theatre: Intermezzi

Intermezzi were comical and musical interludes performed between acts of the Commedia dell'arte in Italy from the 16th century. They were short and entertaining scenes played between the acts of the main play and often included dances, songs, acrobatics, wordplay, and jokes. Intermezzi were highly popular with the Italian public, who quickly embraced this form of interlude.

Intermezzi were performed by masked actors, often accompanied by live music. The actors were experienced comedians of the Commedia dell'arte, who were able to improvise comic dialogues and entertain the audience with their skills. Intermezzi were a cherished source of entertainment for spectators of all ages and backgrounds.

Intermezzi had a significant impact on the development of Italian and European theatre. They influenced the form and content of the Commedia dell'arte, as well as other theatrical forms of the time. Intermezzi also had considerable influence on the music of the time. Italian composers started composing music specifically for intermezzi, leading to the emergence of opera. In fact, the first Italian opera, Jacopo Peri's Dafne, was created in 1597 for an intermezzo.

Intermezzi also had an important influence on European culture in general. Intermezzi were exported to other countries like France and England, where they influenced the development of local theatrical forms. For example, in France, intermezzi were adapted to become entr'actes, which were added to the main plays.

French Theatre: Humanist Tragedies

Humanist tragedies are a genre of theatre that emerged in France during the Renaissance. These plays are characterized by an exploration of philosophical and ethical themes, as well as an interest in humanism and knowledge. Humanist tragedy authors sought to reconcile Christian morality with the ideas of ancient thought.

Humanist tragedies were influenced by the works of the Italian humanist Petrarch, who popularized the idea of a return to the values of ancient Greece. Humanist tragedies were also influenced by the works of the French philosopher Michel de Montaigne, who published essays on subjects such as human nature and the human condition.

The most famous plays of the humanist tragedy genre were written by Pierre Corneille, including «Le Cid» (1637) and «Horace» (1640). These plays depict characters facing complex moral dilemmas and having to choose between their duty and their love, or their loyalty to their family or their country.

Humanist tragedies were also written by other French authors of the time, such as Jean Racine and Voltaire. Racine's plays, such as «Phèdre» (1677), are known for their exploration of themes of passion and guilt, while Voltaire's plays, such as «Zaïre» (1732), are known for their criticism of religion and intolerance.

Humanist tragedies had a significant influence on the development of French and European theatre in general. The plays were popular with the public, who appreciated their exploration of ethical themes and criticism of society and religion. Humanist tragedies were also studied in schools and universities, where they were considered as an example of the successful fusion of Christian and ancient ideas.

French Theatre: Humanist Comedies

Humanist comedies are a genre of French theatre in the 16th century that drew inspiration from humanist philosophy, which advocated freedom of thought and individual fulfillment. These comedies differed from farces and Italian Renaissance comedies, which were more focused on entertainment and comedy.

Humanist comedies were more character-driven plays, where characters were more complex and nuanced, and the purpose was not only to amuse but also to provoke reflection. The aim of humanist comedies was to portray everyday life situations that revealed the flaws and vices of human nature, while showing how characters could overcome them by demonstrating wisdom, humility, and tolerance.

The most famous author of humanist comedies is undoubtedly Molière, whose plays such as «Le Misanthrope» or «L'Avare» have become classics of French literature. In these plays, Molière criticizes the vices of his contemporary society by portraying caricatured characters representing social stereotypes, such as the miserly bourgeois, the pretentious aristocrat, or the cynical intellectual.

But Molière was not the only author of humanist comedies in 16th century France. Other authors, such as Georges de Scudéry, Jean de La Fontaine, Jean Racine, and Pierre Corneille, also wrote plays in this genre. Their plays portrayed characters facing moral dilemmas, such as honor, loyalty, justice, and truth.

The staging of humanist comedies was often more restrained than that of farces and Italian Renaissance comedies. Sets were simple, or even nonexistent, with the focus on the actors' performances and the quality of the text. Actors had to convey emotion and psychological complexity of the characters, using subtle gestures and facial expressions to enhance the play's meaning.

English Theatre: William Shakespeare Life and Works

William Shakespeare is one of the most famous playwrights of all time. Born in 1564 in Stratford-upon-Avon, England, he lived during the Elizabethan era, a period of cultural and artistic renaissance. Shakespeare wrote plays that are still considered classics today, such as «Hamlet», «Romeo and Juliet», «Macbeth», «King Lear», and «Othello».

Shakespeare's life is surrounded by mystery, but it is generally believed that he began his theatrical career in London in the 1590s. He worked as an actor and playwright for the Lord Chamberlain's Men theatre company, which later became the King's Men. Shakespeare was a prolific writer, creating at least 37 plays during his career. He also wrote poems such as «Venus and Adonis» and «The Rape of Lucrece».

Shakespeare's works are renowned for their richness of language, complexity of plot, and characterization of characters. His plays explore universal themes such as love, betrayal, revenge, and politics. His plays have often been adapted for film and television, and are regularly performed in theatres worldwide.

Elizabethan theatre, in which Shakespeare worked, was characterized by a blend of genres including comedy, tragedy, and history. The plays were performed in open-air theatres, with little or no scenery, but with elaborate costumes and abundant use of music and sound effects. The actors were often men, and female roles were played by boys.

Shakespeare wrote in all popular theatre genres of the time, including romantic comedies, tragedies, historical plays, and intricate plot plays. His plays were produced in theatres of all sizes, from small round theatres to large venues such as the Globe Theatre, which was specifically built for Shakespeare's plays.

Shakespeare's style is often considered challenging for modern readers due to the complexity of his language and the richness of cultural references. However, his plays are often studied in schools and universities for their importance in the history of literature and theatre.

In summary, William Shakespeare is one of the most famous and influential playwrights in the history of theatre. His plays are renowned for their richness in language, complexity of plot, and characterization of characters. His work has had a significant influence on theatre and culture in general, and his plays are still performed and studied worldwide.

English Theatre: Elizabethan Theatre

Elizabethan theatre, also known as Elizabethan-Jacobean theatre, is one of the most significant periods in English theatre history. This period covers the late 16th century and the early 17th century, corresponding to the reign of Queen Elizabeth I and her successor, James I. This era was characterized by an explosion of creativity and innovation in the world of theatre, leading to the creation of many literary and dramatic masterpieces.

Elizabethan theatre is often associated with the work of William Shakespeare, who is arguably the most famous and influential author of this period. However, it should not be forgotten that Elizabethan theatre also saw the emergence of other great playwrights such as Christopher Marlowe, Ben Jonson, John Webster, Thomas Middleton, and many others.

One of the most remarkable aspects of Elizabethan theatre is the diversity of genres and dramatic styles that were produced. There were tragic plays, comedies, historical dramas, bloody tragedies, political intrigue plays, social comedies, thesis plays, and more. The themes explored were also highly diverse, ranging from court life to peasant life, from love to war, from politics to religion.

Elizabethan theatre is also known for its scenic and technical innovations. The theaters of the time were often built in a circular or octagonal shape, with an open stage and an audience surrounding the actors from all sides. The sets were often simple, but the costumes were luxurious and colorful. Special effects were also very popular, with battle scenes, smoke effects, supernatural appearances, and more.

Elizabethan theatre was also a popular art form that reached a wide audience. The plays were performed in public theaters, which welcomed spectators from all social classes. The actors were often men, but there were also female performers who played female roles. The plays were often witty and full of humor, with wordplay and delightful dialogue that were highly appreciated by the audience.

Baroque Theatre in Spain

Baroque theatre in Spain is an important period in the history of Spanish theatre that extends from the early 17th century to the late 18th century. This period saw the emergence of a distinctive theatrical style characterized by extravagant aesthetics, dramatic effects, and the use of music and dance.

Baroque theatre in Spain was a reaction to the previous period, the Spanish Golden Age. This period was characterized by a more sober and austere aesthetic focused on the representation of honor, morality, and religion.

Baroque theatre in Spain sought to distinguish itself from this period by creating an extravagant aesthetic filled with contrasts, movements, and dramatic visual effects. This aesthetic was influenced by the baroque art of the time, which sought to dazzle the audience with grand and theatrical works.

One of the most important aspects of Spanish Baroque theatre was the central role of religious and monarchical authorities in the production of spectacles. Indeed, the plays were often commissioned and financed by the Church or the monarchy, who sought to use theatre as a propaganda tool. However, despite this censorship, Baroque theatrical plays were often critical of authorities and social inequalities.

Baroque theatrical plays in Spain were often filled with religious symbols and dramatic representations of the lives of saints and martyrs. The main characters were often kings, queens, nobles, or religious heroes. The plays were also characterized by the use of music, dance, and special effects to create an immersive theatrical experience.

Prominent authors of Baroque theatre in Spain include Lope de Vega, Pedro Calderón de la Barca, and Tirso de Molina. Their plays were often historical dramas or comedies of manners, reflecting the concerns of Spanish society at the time.

Baroque theatre in Spain also saw significant advancements in set designs and costumes, with elaborate and detailed designs that added to the grandeur of the productions. The plays were often performed in covered theatres, which provided a lavish setting for the performances. Actors and actresses also played a vital role in Baroque theatre, with an exaggerated and expressive acting style that reflected the dramatic aesthetic of the period.

Baroque theatre in Spain had a significant influence on the development of theatre in Europe and around the world. This period marked an important stage in the history of Spanish theatre and left a significant legacy that is still evident today.

Classical Theater

The rules of classical theater

The rules of classical theater played a crucial role in the evolution of European theater, particularly in France in the 17th century. They were developed by authors such as Pierre Corneille and Jean Racine and aimed to establish a certain harmony and unity in plays.

The first rule of classical theater is that of the three unities: unity of time, unity of place, and unity of action. Unity of time states that the plot must unfold in one day, allowing the audience to follow the action continuously. Unity of place means that the action must take place in one location or in very close locations, allowing the audience's attention to be focused on the main action. Lastly, unity of action requires that the plot be simple and have a single main storyline, allowing the audience to focus on the main story.

The second rule of classical theater is the rule of decorum, which demands that characters and actions conform to societal norms. This rule required that violent acts and obscene scenes be avoided on stage, as they could offend the public. Characters had to be portrayed in a way that elicited admiration rather than repulsion.

The third rule of classical theater is the rule of verisimilitude, which demands that the plot be plausible and realistic. Actions and dialogues must align with the characteristics of the characters and should not be unrealistic or implausible.

Supernatural or impossible events should be avoided in order to maintain the illusion of reality and allow the audience to immerse themselves in the story.

These rules were widely adopted in France and Europe starting from the 17th century and had a significant influence on the theater of the time. They sought to establish a certain harmony and unity in plays but also limited the creativity of the authors. However, their importance should not be underestimated as they have influenced the way we perceive and appreciate theater today.

It is worth noting that these rules have been criticized over time as they limited the creativity of the authors and often led to overly predictable and stereotypical plays. However, their influence on European theater remains undeniable, and they have been taught in theater schools for several centuries.

Classical Tragedy and Comedy

Classical tragedy and comedy are two distinct forms of theater that emerged in France in the 17th century, during the golden age of French theater. Classical tragedy is characterized by serious subjects and noble characters, while classical comedy is lighter and focuses on everyday life subjects.

Classical tragedy relies on a rigorous dramatic structure based on the rule of the three unities (unity of time, place, and action), which advocates that the action takes place in a single location, within a limited time frame, and revolves around a central action. This rule aims to focus the audience's attention on the plot and characters rather than peripheral details. Prominent tragic authors of the time, such as Pierre Corneille and Jean Racine, also emphasized morality and honor and often used historical figures to illustrate these themes.

Classical comedy, on the other hand, features characters from the middle class, often in funny and absurd situations. Comedy authors, such as Molière, also followed the rigorous dramatic structure of the three unities but allowed for greater freedom in developing characters and situations. Classical comedy also addressed social and political issues, such as critiquing the customs and institutions of the time.

Although classical tragedy and comedy were highly popular theater forms in their time, they also faced criticism. Some accused classical tragedy of being too rigid and artificial, while others considered classical comedy to be too light and superficial.

However, classical tragedy and comedy have had a great influence on European theater and laid the groundwork for many modern theater forms. The rules of rigorous dramatic structure have been adopted by other theater forms, while the themes addressed in classical tragedies and comedies have inspired many subsequent authors.

Great Playwrights: Corneille, Molière, and Racine

The great authors of French classical theater, Corneille, Molière, and Racine, have left their mark on the history of theater and have been considered pillars of the golden age of French theater. Their works have influenced literature, art, and culture for centuries and are still performed and studied worldwide.

Pierre Corneille, born in 1606, is known for creating the genre of classical tragedy in France. He wrote numerous plays, among which the most famous, Le Cid, was first performed in 1637. This play tells the story of love between Rodrigue and Chimène, and the revenge he must take on her father. Corneille is also known for his plays Horace and Cinna, which explore similar themes of love and duty.

Molière, whose real name was Jean-Baptiste Poquelin, was born in 1622 and is considered one of the greatest comedic playwrights of all time. He wrote numerous satirical comedies, among the most famous being Le Misanthrope, Tartuffe, and L'Avare. His plays were often criticized for their social satire and criticism of religious and social hypocrisy of his time. Molière was also a talented actor and often performed in his own plays.

Jean Racine, born in 1639, is known for his classical tragedies, which are often considered more emotional and intimate than those of Corneille. His plays, such as Andromaque, Phèdre, and Britannicus, explore themes of passion, jealousy, and betrayal. Racine also wrote prolifically for the royal court and became the official poet of Louis XIV.

These three authors all wrote during the time of absolute monarchy in France and were influenced by the rules of classical theater, established by the 16th-century Italian playwright, Lodovico Castelvetro. These rules included the unity of time, place, and action, which encouraged playwrights to write plays that took place in one location, over a 24-hour period, and followed a clear plot pattern.

Despite these strict rules, the plays of Corneille, Molière, and Racine were acclaimed for their complexity, characterization, and elaborate literary style. Their works have been studied in schools and universities worldwide and continue to influence modern playwrights.

The Role of Women on Stage

The contribution of women on the theatrical stage has often been underestimated and overlooked in the history of theater. Yet, their role is essential, and their impact considerable. Since ancient times, women have had to overcome many obstacles to perform on stage.

In ancient Greek theater, women were completely excluded from the stage, as their roles were played by men. This practice continued for centuries in other theatrical cultures such as Roman theater, medieval theater, and Renaissance theater.

It was only in the 17th century that women began to play

female roles on stage, but their access was still limited, and their roles often amounted to secondary roles. It was not until the 18th century that their participation on stage became more common. Actresses began to play more significant and complex roles, and entire plays were written specifically for them.

Despite this, women continued to face many challenges to fully express themselves on stage. The patriarchal society of the time viewed women as weak beings incapable of independent thought and action, which hindered them from taking on more significant and complex roles. The prejudices of the time were also reflected in stage design, where costumes and sets were often designed to reinforce the idea of women as sexual objects or fragile creatures.

However, despite these challenges, some women managed to establish themselves on stage and play major roles in the history of theater. For example, Molière often wrote strong roles for women, such as those of Célimène in Le Misanthrope or Elvire in Don Juan. In the 18th century, French actress Adrienne Lecouvreur was a pioneer in playing leading roles in significant plays, despite opposition from male critics of the time.

In the 19th century, actresses continued to break barriers by playing more complex roles and engaging in plays that tackled more serious subjects. Sarah Bernhardt, a renowned French actress, played male roles in some plays and even performed dangerous stunts on stage, which contributed to changing the image of women in theater.

In the 20th century, women continued to make significant strides on the stage. The feminist movement of the 1960s and 1970s advocated for gender equality in all areas, including theater. Women began to write, direct, and produce their own plays, allowing them to take control of their own storytelling and tell stories that were uniquely theirs. Augusto Boal's Theater of the Oppressed also provided women with a platform to express their voice and experience.

Despite these advancements, women still face obstacles on the theatrical stage. Male roles prevail, and actresses are often relegated to secondary roles or gender stereotypes. Women also face beauty and physical stereotypes, which can impact their theater careers.

However, many actresses and artists continue to work to break down these barriers and create positive change in the theater industry. Plays that highlight women's stories, written and directed by women, have gained popularity and won prestigious awards. Women also hold key positions in the theater industry, such as theater directors, directors, and set designers.

French Theater of the 17th Century

French theater of the 17th century is often considered the golden age of French theater, particularly thanks to the great works of playwrights such as Corneille, Molière, and Racine. It was a time when theater took a central place in French culture and became a highly appreciated and respected art form.

French theater of the 17th century was influenced by classicism and the strict rules of classical tragedy. Plays were characterized by noble characters, elaborate dialogues, and a rigorous dramatic structure with five acts. Playwrights were also heavily influenced by Antiquity, especially Greek tragedies.

French theater of the 17th century was marked by the rivalry between the two greatest playwrights of the time, Pierre Corneille and Jean Racine. Corneille wrote plays such as Le Cid, Horace, and Cinna, which were hailed for their grandeur and eloquence. Racine, on the other hand, wrote tragedies such as Phèdre, Britannicus, and Andromaque, which were praised for their emotional intensity and complex psychology.

French theater of the 17th century was also influenced by the work of Molière, who wrote comedies such as Le Misanthrope, Tartuffe, and L'Avare. Molière's plays were acclaimed for their social satire and incisive humor, as well as for their ability to challenge the norms of the time.

French theater of the 17th century was characterized by the significant role of women on stage. Actresses began to play important roles and were acclaimed for their talent and beauty. Women also started playing male roles, as plays were written for a limited number of characters and actors were often scarce.

French theater of the 17th century had a significant impact on world theater, particularly on English theater. Shakespeare's plays were translated into French and performed in France, influencing the work of French playwrights such as Corneille and Racine. Molière's plays were also performed in England and influenced subsequent English comedies.

The Spanish Theater of the Golden Age

The Spanish theater of the Golden Age was one of the most important and influential periods in the history of European theater. This period spanned from the 16th to the 17th century and corresponded to the golden age of Spanish culture, characterized by artistic effervescence and unprecedented cultural richness.

The Spanish theater of the Golden Age was primarily marked by two genres: la comedia and la tragedia. La comedia was a comedic play, often in prose, while la tragedia was a more serious play, often in verse.

The most famous playwright of this period was Lope de Vega, who wrote over 1500 plays. His plays were often comedies, but he also wrote tragedies and historical plays. He introduced new forms of storytelling in Spanish theater, including complex love intrigues and the use of crowd scenes to add action and emotion.

Another important playwright of this period was Pedro Calderón de la Barca, who wrote tragic and comedic plays. His plays often revolved around religious and philosophical themes and were written in verse.

The Spanish theater of the Golden Age was also characterized by a distinctive baroque style, which manifested in sets, costumes, and special effects. The theaters of the time were often decorated with architectural elements such as columns and arches, and actors wore sumptuous and elaborate costumes.

The Spanish theater of the Golden Age had a great influence on European theater and contributed to the evolution of modern theater. Spanish playwrights introduced new forms of storytelling, innovative staging techniques, and styles of acting that inspired many European artists.

English Theater of the Restoration

English theater of the Restoration was an exciting and dynamic period in the history of British theater. After the forced closure of theaters by Oliver Cromwell during the Commonwealth period, the Restoration of the monarchy under Charles II saw the reopening of theaters in 1660. This period marked the beginning of an unprecedented theatrical revival, which introduced new genres, actors, playwrights, and forms of expression.

One of the most notable features of English theater of the Restoration was the explosion of new play genres. The comedy of manners was particularly popular during this time, featuring satirical portrayals of love intrigues and social conflicts. Characters were often exaggerated caricatures, and the language used was often crude and vulgar. The plays were often immoral and focused on sexuality, sparking public debates about the morals of society at the time.

However, there were also other important genres such as sentimental comedy, heroic tragedy, serious drama, and heroic drama, all of which were popular during this period. These plays were often more serious than the comedies of manners and tackled subjects such as honor, morality, and virtue.

Another significant characteristic of English theater of the Restoration was the arrival of the first professional actresses, who had previously been prohibited from performing on stage. Nell Gwyn and Anne Bracegirdle were two of the most famous actresses of the time and paved the way for many others who followed.

Restoration playwrights also left their mark on the history of English theater. William Wycherley, George Etherege, John Dryden, and William Congreve are some of the greatest names of this period. Their plays influenced British theater for centuries and are still regularly performed today. Their plays were often immoral and provocative, but they were also innovative and groundbreaking.

In addition to new genres, new actors, and new playwrights, English theater of the Restoration also saw the emergence of new acting styles. Actors were often chosen for their appearance rather than their acting skills, and plays were often performed in an exaggerated and stylized manner.

Theatre in the 18th and 19th Century

Bourgeois Drama

Bourgeois drama was a form of theatre that emerged in France in the 18th century, at a time when the bourgeoisie was growing as an increasingly powerful economic and political force in society. This theatrical genre was characterized by plays that featured characters from the middle class, often facing everyday problems such as love, marriage, family, career, money, and morality. The plays were typically written in verse and were intended to be performed in private or public theaters in the city.

Bourgeois drama was heavily influenced by opera-comique and comedy, which had been popular among French audiences in previous centuries. However, bourgeois drama distinguished itself from these genres through its realistic and moralistic treatment of social issues, making it both entertaining and instructive.

The success of bourgeois drama extended beyond France, reaching other European countries such as Germany, England, and Italy. However, its impact was particularly strong in France, where it remained popular until the end of the 19th century.

Bourgeois drama was criticized by some contemporaries for its lack of originality and predictability, as well as its conservative and moralizing nature. However, it was also appreciated for its realistic portrayal of characters and situations, which allowed the audience to identify and reflect on the social issues of their time.

Despite the criticism, bourgeois drama was an important form of theatre that reflected the values and concerns of the emerging middle class in French society in the 18th century. It also influenced other forms of theatre, such as the realistic and naturalistic theatre of the 19th century, which continued to explore the themes and motifs introduced by bourgeois drama. The genre also contributed to the richness and diversity of French theatrical heritage.

For example, French playwright Marivaux created several plays that influenced the bourgeois drama genre, such as «The Game of Love and Chance» (1730) and «False Confidences» (1737). These plays featured characters from the middle class navigating through difficult and complex situations, while addressing important moral and social questions.

Similarly, German playwright Gotthold Ephraim Lessing wrote plays such as «Miss Sara Sampson» (1755) and «Emilia Galotti» (1772), which also explored the themes and motifs of bourgeois drama, such as marriage, honor, virtue, and social class.

Comedy of Manners

Comedy of manners is a theatrical genre with a long history that continues to captivate audiences. It is particularly interesting because it allows for the satirical portrayal of social behaviors and values while entertaining the audience. This genre focuses on the vices and flaws of society and its members, often using ridicule and humor to critique them.

The origins of comedy of manners can be traced back to ancient Greece, where Aristophanes wrote satirical plays to denounce the faults of Athenian society. In the Middle Ages, playwrights used comedy of manners to criticize the customs and beliefs of their time. This tradition continued during the Renaissance in Italy, where Commedia dell'arte plays often used comedy to expose abuses of power and social inequalities.

However, it was in 17th and 18th century France that comedy of manners reached its peak. Playwrights of the time, such as Molière, Marivaux, and Beaumarchais, used this genre to denounce the vices and social inequalities of their time. Molière, for example, is famous for his comedies of manners such as «The Misanthrope» and «Tartuffe,» which highlight the faults of French aristocratic society in the 17th century. Marivaux, on the other hand, used comedy of manners to highlight gender and social class inequalities, as seen in «The Game of Love and Chance.» Beaumarchais, with his trilogy «The Barber of Seville,» «The Marriage of Figaro,» and «The Guilty Mother,» also used comedy of manners to critique contemporary aristocratic society, particularly by denouncing abuses of power and social inequalities.

In England, the comedy of manners genre was used to critique the rigidity of Victorian society. Playwrights like Oscar Wilde wrote plays that entertained the audience while criticizing the social norms and behaviors of the time, such as «The Importance of Being Earnest.»

Today, comedy of manners continues to be a popular genre in theatre, as it allows for laughter while making the audience reflect on the behaviors and values of contemporary society. Plays such as «Le Prénom» by Matthieu Delaporte and Alexandre de la Patellière or «The Truth Game» by Florian Zeller are examples of contemporary comedy of manners that continue to critique society and its flaws.

Melodrama and Vaudeville

Melodrama and vaudeville are two forms of theatre that were highly successful in France and Europe in the late 18th and 19th centuries. Melodrama is a dramatic theatrical genre characterized by the abundant use of music, dance, and scenic effects to evoke strong emotions in the audience. Vaudeville, on the other hand, is a light and humorous comedy that relies on complex plots, misunderstandings, and wordplay to entertain the audience.

Melodrama originated in France in the late 18th century and enjoyed great success throughout Europe in the 19th century. Melodramas were often based on popular novels, stories of impossible love, exotic adventures, or dramatic historical events. The characters in melodramas were often heroes or heroines who had to overcome obstacles to achieve their goals, and the situations were often punctuated with songs, dances, and spectacular action scenes. Melodrama was popular among all social classes and contributed to the popularization of theatre among a wider audience.

Vaudeville also originated in France in the late 18th century and enjoyed great success in Parisian theaters throughout the 19th century. Vaudevilles were light and playful comedies that relied on complex plots, misunderstandings, and wordplay to entertain the audience. The characters in vaudeville were often bourgeois, servants, or comic characters who found themselves in ludicrous and absurd situations. Vaudeville was popular among all social classes and contributed to the popularization of theatre among a wider audience.

Although melodrama and vaudeville are different forms of theatre, they share common characteristics. Both forms rely on simple and clear plots that are easy for the audience to follow. Both forms also use spectacular scenic effects to evoke strong emotions in the audience. Both forms also contributed to the popularization of theatre among a wider audience.

Great Playwrights: Marivaux, Beaumarchais, and Voltaire

The playwrights Marivaux, Beaumarchais, and Voltaire are iconic figures in 18th-century French theatre. Their works have left an indelible mark on the history of French theatre by contributing to the evolution of dramatic genres and introducing new codes and aesthetics.

Marivaux is considered the master of light and sophisticated comedy. His plays are gems of finesse and intelligence, where the games of love and seduction are subtly staged. His dialogues are elegant and refined, rich in subtleties and nuances. Marivaux created complex characters who navigate delicate social situations. He skillfully uses irony and humor to expose the absurdities of his era's society while preserving a certain lightness and a touch of poetry.

Beaumarchais, on the other hand, is famous for his trilogy «The Barber of Seville,» «The Marriage of Figaro,» and «The Guilty Mother.» His plays are true gems of French dramatic literature, featuring a fast-paced succession of linguistic games, misunderstandings, and plot twists. But beyond humor and wit, Beaumarchais' plays are social critiques that denounce the inequalities and injustices of his time. He portrays strong characters who fight for their freedom and dignity. His hero, Figaro, has become a symbol of critical thinking and resistance against oppression.

Voltaire, for his part, is a multifaceted author who wrote plays, novels, essays, and poems. His theatre, influenced by French classicism, depicts noble and heroic characters who fight for justice and truth. His most famous plays, such as «Candide» and «The Ingenu,» are social satires where he denounces abuses of power and societal hypocrisies. Voltaire is a committed author who uses satire and irony to criticize the vices of his time.

These three playwrights have left a lasting impact on French theatre with their creative genius and audacity. Their plays have been performed on stages worldwide and have inspired numerous artists and writers. Marivaux, Beaumarchais, and Voltaire were able to renew the dramatic genre by introducing new codes and aesthetics while preserving the richness and diversity of the French theatrical heritage. Their plays, still relevant and compelling, continue to fascinate and enchant modern audiences.

The Birth of Realistic and Naturalistic Theatre

The birth of realistic and naturalistic theatre marked a break from previous theatrical forms. Realistic and naturalistic theatre, which emerged in the late 19th century, aimed to represent life as it truly is, featuring ordinary characters and realistic situations. Authors of this era broke away from classical and romantic theatre conventions, introducing social and political themes, exploring the darkest aspects of existence, and creating complex and nuanced characters.

The realistic movement emerged in France in the 1850s with authors such as Gustave Flaubert and Emile Zola, who wrote realistic novels portraying the daily lives of the working class. In theatre, the realistic movement manifested itself through playwrights such as Alexandre Dumas fils, who wrote «The Lady of the Camellias» in 1852, a play that was a resounding success due to its realistic treatment of love and death.

The naturalistic movement, on the other hand, appeared in the late 1870s in France. Naturalistic authors aimed to explore the social, economic, and biological determinisms that shape characters' lives. Naturalistic plays were often dark and despairing, featuring characters suffering from mental illness, poverty, or physical ailments. The most famous naturalistic plays are those of Henrik Ibsen, such as «A Doll's House» (1879), which was a sharp critique of patriarchal society and caused a great scandal at its first performance.

Realistic and naturalistic theatre also brought significant technical changes. Sets and costumes were simplified to portray reality more authentically. Actors also adopted a more natural style, focusing on expressing emotional truth rather than grandiosity and exaggeration. This approach paved the way for new acting techniques, such as Stanislavski's method, which influenced many actors and directors in the 20th century.

Modern Theatre (20th Century)

The Theatre of the Absurd and Existentialism

The Theatre of the Absurd and Existentialism is a theatrical movement that emerged in Europe in the 1950s and revolutionized the theater scene. This movement is part of the existentialist trend, a philosophical movement that advocates for individual existence, freedom, and personal responsibility.

The Theatre of the Absurd is characterized by the use of seemingly illogical dialogues, absurd situations, and disoriented characters searching for meaning in their existence. This form of theater rejects traditional logic and aims to disrupt established theatrical conventions.

Irish playwright Samuel Beckett is considered one of the pioneers of the Theatre of the Absurd. His plays, such as «Waiting for Godot» and «Endgame,» depict characters lost in a senseless world, desperately seeking meaning in their existence. Beckett uses minimalist dialogue, stripped-down staging, and caricatured characters to create an absurd and oppressive universe.

Existentialist theatre, on the other hand, focuses on human existence and the search for meaning. Plays belonging to this movement portray characters who confront the limits of their existence and strive to find purpose in life. Authors within this movement often explore fundamental philosophical questions of human existence, such as anguish, solitude, death, and freedom.

French playwright Jean-Paul Sartre is one of the main representatives of existentialist theater. His plays, such as «No Exit» and «Dirty Hands,» depict characters faced with moral choices and situations that challenge their very existence. Sartre uses sharp dialogue and complex characters to explore the existential dilemmas that individuals confront.

The Theatre of the Absurd and Existentialism has greatly influenced the theatrical world and has inspired numerous playwrights and directors. These movements have contributed to a revolution in theater by challenging established conventions and exploring new artistic territories.

Major authors: Beckett, Ionesco, and Genet

The literary and artistic movements of the Absurd and Existentialism have had a significant impact on 20th-century theater. They have questioned traditional genre conventions and explored universal themes such as life, death, solitude, and the human condition. Major authors within these movements have employed innovative techniques to convey their worldview, creating unsettling characters and surreal dialogues that evoke the absurdity of existence.

Samuel Beckett is considered one of the founders of the Absurd, and his most famous work, «Waiting for Godot,» has become a cornerstone of modern theater. The characters in his plays often find themselves in hopeless situations, desperately searching for meaning in their existence. «Endgame» is another poignant example of Beckett's vision of human life.

Eugène Ionesco also had a significant influence on the Absurd movement. His play «The Bald Soprano» became a symbol of life's absurdity. The play is set in a universe where characters seem unable to communicate and where language itself appears to be emptied of meaning. «Rhinoceros» is another important work by Ionesco, portraying a town overrun by rhinoceroses that symbolize the rise of totalitarianism.

Jean Genet, on the other hand, focused more on existentialism and explored the complexities of human nature, including violence, sexuality, and death. His play «The Maids» tells the story of two sisters planning the murder of their mistress, revealing their own alienation and despair in the face of their existence.

These authors share a common use of poetic and vivid language to express their ideas and evoke the deep emotions of their characters. Their works have also been influenced by literary and artistic movements of their time, such as existentialism and surrealism, as well as by political and social events of their era.

The significance of the Absurd and Existentialist movements in 20th-century theater lies in their pushing of boundaries and challenging of traditional conventions. They offered new ways of perceiving the world and inspired writers and artists who followed in their footsteps.

Epic Theatre and Theatre of Engagement

Epic Theatre and Theatre of Engagement are two theatrical movements that emerged in the early 20th century as reactions to the crisis of society and the rise of fascism and Nazism in Europe. Both movements aim to raise awareness among audiences and encourage critical reflection on social and political issues of the time.

Epic Theatre, developed by Bertolt Brecht, is characterized by its didactic and consciousness-raising nature. This type of theater utilizes techniques to break the theatrical illusion and encourage the audience to take a critical distance from the play. The characters are not portrayed realistically but rather as archetypes. Dialogues are written in a way that prevents the audience from identifying with the characters but rather prompts them to analyze the situations presented.

The Theatre of Engagement, on the other hand, is a politically and socially engaged theater. Its emergence stemmed from the desire to use theater as a tool in the struggle against social and political injustices. It employs forms of popular theater to reach a broad audience and create a movement of liberation. This type of theater was popularized by Augusto Boal and his Theatre of the Oppressed.

Both of these theatrical movements share the aim of awakening the political consciousness of the audience and motivating them to take action in transforming society. They have had a significant impact on the history of theater and have inspired many artists worldwide.

However, despite their importance and influence, Epic Theatre and Theatre of Engagement have also faced criticism. Some have argued that these movements can be overly didactic and do not leave space for emotion and poetry. Others believe that their approach is too simplistic and fails to consider the complexity of social and political issues.

Despite these criticisms, Epic Theatre and Theatre of Engagement have left a mark on theater history and continue to inspire socially engaged artists today. They have proven that theater can be a powerful tool for raising awareness and fighting against social and political injustices.

Major authors: Brecht, Sartre, and Weiss

In the world of theater, the notions of epic theater and theater of engagement were introduced by authors who sought to use the stage to criticize society, denounce inequalities, and promote social change. Among the major authors of this trend, we can mention Bertolt Brecht, Jean-Paul Sartre, and Peter Weiss.

Bertolt Brecht is undoubtedly one of the most famous playwrights of epic theater and engagement. Brecht sought to actively involve the audience in his plays, using techniques such as distancing and fragmented staging to break traditional theatrical illusions and prompt audiences to reflect on the social and political themes of his works. In plays like «Life of Galileo» and «Mother Courage and Her Children,» Brecht used metaphors and analogies to critique authoritarian political regimes and encourage social engagement. He also incorporated songs in his plays, which served to reinforce the social and political themes of his works.

Jean-Paul Sartre, the renowned French writer, philosopher, and playwright, is known for his socially and politically engaged works. In his plays, Sartre explored issues such as class struggle, war, freedom, and human existence. He was particularly known for his play «No Exit,» in which he critically examines the role some communists played in the French Resistance during World War II. Sartre was also a staunch advocate for existentialism, a philosophy emphasizing individual freedom and responsibility that influenced his theatrical vision.

Peter Weiss, a Swedish-German playwright, is famous for politically engaged plays like «The Investigation,» which deals with the Auschwitz trials, and «Marat/Sade,» which combines elements of epic theater, engaged theater, and theater of cruelty. Weiss sought to denounce social and political injustices in his plays and to encourage audiences to take action for positive change. In «The Investigation,» Weiss used fragmented storytelling to reflect the confusion and brutality of the Nazi regime and prompt the audience to reflect on the consequences of state violence.

These three authors used theater to stimulate reflection and social action by addressing political and social issues. Their plays became powerful tools for critiquing authoritarian regimes, inequalities, and injustices, and for encouraging audiences to engage in positive societal change.

Theatre of the Intimate and Everyday Life

Theatre of the Intimate and Everyday Life is a form of theater that explores the deepest aspects of human beings by emphasizing the personal stories and experiences of actors and audiences. This type of theater is often performed in intimate and informal settings, such as café-theaters, living rooms, or even public spaces.

Theatre of the Intimate and Everyday Life focuses on universal themes of human existence, such as love, family, death, loss, identity, and the search for meaning. It is a highly personal form of theater that often touches audiences in a deeper and more emotional way than other forms of theater.

Theatre of the Intimate and Everyday Life is characterized by a close proximity between actors and the audience. Actors often sit or stand very close to the audience, creating an intimate and warm atmosphere. Plays are often based on improvisations or short scenes, allowing actors to react spontaneously to the audience's reactions.

This form of theater is vastly different from large-scale theater productions with grand sets and special effects. Instead, Theatre of the Intimate and Everyday Life focuses on simplicity and authenticity. Sets are often minimal or non-existent, and costumes are often everyday clothes.

Theatre of the Intimate and Everyday Life is often associated with the Theatre of the Oppressed movement developed by Brazilian theorist Augusto Boal. This movement emphasizes the importance of interaction and audience participation in theater, using theater as a tool for social transformation.

In conclusion, Theatre of the Intimate and Everyday Life is a form of theater that prioritizes authenticity, simplicity, and closeness between actors and the audience. It is a form of theater that often deeply touches spectators by exploring universal themes of human existence.

Augusto Boal's Theatre of the Oppressed

Augusto Boal's Theatre of the Oppressed is a method of social and political theater aimed at creating interactive performances that raise awareness of situations of oppression, discrimination, and injustice. This method was developed in Brazil in the 1960s by Boal, a playwright, director, and political activist.

Boal was born in Rio de Janeiro in 1931. From a young age, he witnessed social inequalities and political violence. During his theater studies, he began questioning the passive role of spectators and started searching for ways to involve them in the theatrical creation process. This quest led him to develop his method of Theatre of the Oppressed.

Theatre of the Oppressed uses techniques such as «forum theatre,» «image theatre,» and «invisible theatre» to encourage spectators to become active participants by replacing actors on stage and creatively experimenting with real-life problem-solving.

«Forum theatre,» for example, involves a dialogue between

actors and spectators, during which spectators can take the place of actors in order to try and find solutions to the issues presented on stage. In «invisible theatre,» the actors perform scenes from everyday life, and spectators are invited to intervene and propose solutions.

Boal's method was born out of frustration with the powerlessness of passive spectators in traditional theater. He believed that theater should be a tool for social change and that spectators should be involved in finding solutions to social problems.

Theatre of the Oppressed has been used in diverse contexts, ranging from political conflicts to public health issues and the fight against racism and sexism. It has also inspired numerous artists and activists worldwide.

In conclusion, Theatre of the Oppressed is an engaged and interactive theater method that aims to stimulate thought and social action in its audience. It is a fascinating example of using theater as a tool for social and political change, demonstrating how artists can contribute to societal transformation. Theatre of the Oppressed has also been adapted for use in educational and training contexts, helping individuals develop their creativity, critical thinking, and problem-solving skills.

Innovations in Stage and Theatrical Design in Modern Theatre

In the 20th century, theater experienced unprecedented innovations in stage and theatrical design, pushing the boundaries of dramatic art and creating new forms of expression. Technological advancements, the development of new artistic movements, and social revolution all contributed to these innovations.

One of the most significant advancements in modern theater was the use of technology to create special effects, sets, and costumes that were previously unimaginable. Advances in lighting, sound, video projection, and special effects enabled the creation of immersive stage environments and real-time transformation of sets.

The emergence of new artistic movements, such as surrealism, Dadaism, and futurism, also had a significant impact on modern theater. These movements challenged traditional artistic norms and pushed artists to experiment with innovative techniques and forms of representation.

Another important stage innovation was the use of the actor's body as an instrument of representation. Movements like Augusto Boal's Theatre of the Oppressed encouraged actors to use their bodies and voices creatively to explore important social and political issues.

Modern theater also witnessed the emergence of new forms of representation, such as street theater, immersive and interactive theater, and experimental theater. These forms of theater broke away from traditional stage conventions and encouraged audiences to become active participants in the performance process.

Finally, modern theater also saw a diversification of audiences and represented subjects. Social, political, and cultural issues became increasingly common themes in theatrical plays, and productions were often adapted to reach broader and more diverse audiences.

In conclusion, the stage and theatrical design innovations in modern theater pushed the boundaries of dramatic art and created new forms of expression. Technology, artistic movements, new forms of representation, and audience and subject diversification all contributed to this evolution.

Contemporary Theatre

Postmodern Theatre

Postmodern theatre is an artistic movement that emerged in the 1960s and challenges traditional theatrical conventions. It is characterized by a break with established norms and an exploration of new aesthetic, narrative, and structural concepts. Postmodern artists have sought to deconstruct linear narratives and question hierarchies of gender and power.

One of the most important characteristics of postmodern theatre is its approach to staging. Unlike traditional productions, which often aim to create an illusion of reality, postmodern theatre highlights its own artificiality. Staging is often non-linear and fragmented, with overlapping and juxtaposed elements. Actors may also interact directly with the audience, breaking the fourth wall that normally separates performers from spectators.

Postmodern productions are also often marked by the use of collage techniques. Artists frequently combine different theatrical elements, such as excerpts from literary texts, visual images, and sound elements, to create hybrid and multidisciplinary works.

Another significant aspect of postmodern theatre is its political and social engagement. Postmodern productions have often sought to question established social norms and explore themes such as gender identity, race, sexuality, and social class. Postmodern artists have frequently used theatre as a tool to challenge existing power structures and promote social change.

Finally, postmodern theatre has also been marked by a questioning of the very notion of authorship. Postmodern productions are often collaborative, with contributions from multiple artists, including actors, directors, and set designers. This approach highlights the collective nature of theatre and challenges the idea that a singular author is responsible for creating a theatrical work.

Immersive and Interactive Theatre

Immersive and interactive theatre is a form of theatre that provides a unique and immersive experience for the audience. This form of theatre allows the audience to have a more immersive and interactive theatrical experience compared to traditional theatre, where the audience is usually seated in a space and watches a play unfold on a stage in front of them.

In immersive and interactive theatre, spectators are often invited to move through different spaces where the play takes place, explore the sets, interact with the actors, and actively participate in the action of the play. They may be asked to solve puzzles, discover clues, make decisions that will impact the course of the play, or even play a role in the play.

This form of theatre offers a unique and immersive experience for the audience, who is immersed in a universe specifically created for the play and can directly interact with the actors. This allows the audience to feel more involved in the story and better understand the stakes of the play.

Immersive and interactive theatre can take various forms. Some productions are staged in unconventional spaces, such as warehouses or abandoned factories, to provide the audience with an even more immersive experience. Other productions are staged in traditional theatres but incorporate technologies such as virtual reality or augmented reality to add an additional dimension to the experience.

Immersive and interactive theatre is becoming increasingly popular, with productions like «Sleep No More» in New York and «The Drowned Man» in London enjoying great success with audiences. However, this form of theatre is often more complex and expensive to produce than traditional theatre due to higher production costs and greater technical and logistical requirements.

Moreover, this form of theatre may require different skills from actors, who must be able to interact with the audience and work in a more open and less controlled environment. Directors and designers also need to work differently to create an immersive and realistic environment for the audience.

Immersive and interactive theatre offers a more immersive and participatory experience for the audience, which can be particularly appealing to spectators looking for a more immersive and interactive theatre experience. It also allows artists to push the boundaries of their art and create unique and unforgettable theatrical experiences.

Technical and Aesthetic Aspects of Theatre

Genres and Styles

New forms of theatrical representation have emerged in recent decades and have transformed the way audiences perceive theatre. These new forms explore the boundaries of dramatic art by using cutting-edge technologies, interactive methods, and innovative performance techniques.

One of the most striking forms is immersive and interactive theatre. In this type of performance, spectators are involved in the story by being placed within the environment of the show. They can interact with the actors, explore the set designs, and participate in the action of the story. This type of theatre allows spectators to become active participants, rather than mere passive observers.

Another form that has gained popularity is digital theatre. This form utilizes advanced technologies such as virtual reality, 360-degree video, and multimedia projection to create unique visual and auditory experiences. The audience is transported into imaginary worlds that seem real but are actually created by technology.

Participatory theatre is also trending. In this form, actors and spectators work together to create a performance. Actors may request the audience's help to improvise scenes or solve problems within the story. The audience is encouraged to provide feedback on the performance and interact with the actors during breaks.

Documentary theatre is another emerging form. In this type of performance, actors use real testimonies and documents to tell a story. Actors portray roles based on real people, while excerpts of documents such as audio and video recordings are projected on stage. This form of theatre explores social and political issues in a highly immersive and revealing manner.

Finally, street theatre is a form that utilizes public spaces to tell a story. Performances take place on streets, parks, and public squares, often involving street artists such as acrobats, jugglers, and musicians. This form of theatre is accessible to all passersby, allowing artists to reach a wider and more diverse audience.

Dramatic Structure

The dramatic structure is an essential element of theatre, as it gives coherence to the play, advances the plot, and captivates the audience's interest. It consists of several key elements, such as character introductions, exposition of the plot, rising action, climax, denouement, and epilogue.

Character introductions are a crucial element of the dramatic structure because characters drive the plot and must be understandable and relatable to the audience. The playwright must describe the characters clearly and precisely, presenting their personality, motivations, and relationships with other characters. To achieve this, the playwright can use dialogues, monologues, gestures, and actions to allow the audience to discover the characters' personalities.

The exposition of the plot is also an important element of the dramatic structure, as it allows the audience to understand the play's plot and discover the stakes and obstacles that the characters will have to overcome. This exposition can be presented in various ways, but it must be coherent and understandable. To achieve this, the playwright can use dialogues, monologues, or action scenes to provide important information about the plot.

The rising action is a crucial phase of the dramatic structure, representing the progression of the plot, the increase in dramatic tension, and the escalation of conflicts between characters. The rising action must be progressive, with moments of tension and moments of respite, to maintain the audience's attention. To achieve this, the playwright can use plot twists, conflicts between characters, and action scenes to increase the dramatic tension.

The climax of the play is the moment when the plot reaches its peak. It is the most intense moment of the play, where conflicts are resolved and stakes are clarified. This moment must be memorable and satisfying for the audience. To achieve this, the playwright can use action scenes, plot twists, or revelations to create a strong moment in the play.

The denouement and epilogue represent the end of the play. The denouement is the final resolution of the plot, while the epilogue provides a conclusion to the characters and the story. These moments must be well-crafted to allow for a satisfying ending to the play. To achieve this, the playwright can use dialogues, monologues, or action scenes to provide a resolution to the plot and the characters.

Stage Space and Set Designs

Stage space is one of the key elements of theatre. It is the space in which the action of the play unfolds and where actors interact with the set and the audience. Stage space can vary greatly depending on different theatrical eras, styles, and cultures. Set designs, on the other hand, play a crucial role in creating the atmosphere and ambiance of the play, as well as in identifying the characters and locations.

In early forms of theatre, stage space was often an open space, such as a village square or a field, where actors interacted with the audience. Set designs were often simple and made of natural materials such as branches, stones, or leaves. Over time, stage space developed into an enclosed space, usually an elevated stage with a backdrop and sides.

In Greek theatre, stage space was often a large circle called the orchestra, where actors performed. Set designs were often painted backdrops representing landscapes or buildings, while props were simple objects such as chairs, tables, or weapons.

In Roman theatre, stage space was more complex, with a rectangular raised stage and wings on each side. Set designs were often elaborate wooden structures representing buildings or landscapes, while props were more elaborate and included objects such as chariots, thrones, or statues.

In the Middle Ages, set designs were often rudimentary, as plays were performed in places such as churches or public squares. Props were also simple, such as wooden sticks or swords. As theatre developed further, set designs became more elaborate, with props such as furniture, fabrics, and stage objects.

In the 17th century, set designs were often grand, depicting complex landscapes or buildings. Props were also elaborate, often made of gold or silver. Actors were often dressed in lavish costumes, and plays were performed in ostentatiously decorated theatres.

In the 20th century, theatre underwent a radical evolution in terms of stage space and set designs. Set designs were simplified and stylized to reflect new theatrical movements such as absurd theatre and intimate theatre. Props were also simplified, and costumes were streamlined and modernized. Plays were performed in more intimate spaces such as theatre studios and art galleries, rather than large theatres. Stage innovations also allowed for more impressive visual and auditory effects, with the use of video projections, live music, and innovative staging techniques.

Today, stage space and set designs are used to create an immersive experience for the audience. Plays can be performed in unconventional spaces such as warehouses, parks, or museums to create a specific ambiance. Set designs can also be designed to be interactive, allowing actors and the audience to mingle and immerse themselves in the story.

Stage Direction Approach

Stage direction is a crucial element of theatrical production. It is the creative and collaborative process that translates the director's vision into an immersive and coherent theatrical experience for the audience.

Stage direction involves the creation of stage space, directing actors, the use of lighting and sound, as well as managing costumes and props. All these elements are carefully chosen to reflect the era, location, and social context of the story, and are then coordinated to create a coherent and immersive atmosphere that engages the audience in the world of the play.

To succeed in stage direction, the director must have a clear vision of the story they want to tell. They must be able to communicate this vision to other members of the creative team to create a visual, auditory, and physical representation that aligns with their vision. The choice of set designs, costumes, props, lighting, and sound are all crucial elements in creating the atmosphere and tone of the play. They can add an additional dimension to the performance, creating dramatic effects and enhancing the overall atmosphere of the play.

Directing actors is also a key element of stage direction. The director must be able to guide actors in accurately embodying the characters of the play. They must be able to clearly communicate their vision to the actors and help them find their place within the world of the play. They must also be able to adjust the actors' performances to ensure that their acting is consistent with the tone of the play.

Furthermore, stage direction often involves creating choreography or complex staging for action scenes or crowd scenes. This requires careful coordination between the director, the actors, and the stage technicians.

Lastly, the director must be able to effectively manage the time, resources, and budget available for the production. They must be able to make informed decisions to maximize the impact of each element of the production while respecting budgetary and time constraints.

The Art of Interpretation and Acting Techniques

Interpretation is the cornerstone of theatre, as it allows actors to bring characters to life and effectively communicate the story to the audience. To successfully interpret a character convincingly, an actor must understand their motivations, emotions, actions, and the intentions of the playwright. In this section, we will explore the acting techniques used by actors to bring characters to life and tell the story.

Preparation is key to successful interpretation. Actors must understand the psychology of their character and the dynamics of the play as a whole. They must also understand the tone, style, and intention of the playwright. Once actors have a clear understanding of their character, they can begin using various acting techniques to bring their performance to life.

Physical expression is a key technique used by actors to convey the emotions of their character. Actors must be aware of their posture, movement, and gestures, which can reveal a lot about the character they are portraying. Facial expression is also important, as it can convey subtle emotions to the audience.

Voice is a powerful tool for actors. The tone, speed, and volume of the voice can convey the emotions, motivations, and intentions of the character. Actors must also be aware of their diction and articulation, so that the audience can clearly understand what they are saying.

Emotional connection is another important technique used by actors. To successfully interpret a character, actors must be able to emotionally connect with the character and the story. Actors can use their own experiences to understand the emotions of their character and convey these emotions to the audience authentically.

Spontaneity is also important for successful interpretation. Actors must be able to react spontaneously to other actors and situations on stage, while remaining true to their character. Actors can use improvisation to develop this ability.

Finally, concentration and stage presence are essential for successful interpretation. Actors must be able to remain focused on their character and the story, even in the presence of distractions or technical issues. They must also be present on stage, establishing a connection with the audience and creating a collaborative atmosphere.

Training Schools and Great Actors in History

Actor training has been an essential element of theatre since ancient times. Over the centuries, training schools have evolved to meet the changing needs of actors and directors while preserving theatrical traditions.

One of the earliest actor training schools was Aristotle's school, where students learned techniques for interpreting tragedy and comedy. In the Middle Ages, actors learned their craft on the job, working with itinerant companies. It was only during the Renaissance that training schools began to appear in Europe.

One of the most famous schools of the Renaissance was the Commedia dell'arte in Italy, which was based on improvisation and the creation of stereotypical characters. Actors learned to improvise using masks and costumes, and were often hired to perform in plays written by famous playwrights.

In the 17th century, the French training school had become the reference for European actors. Actors learned techniques of diction, gesture, and posture, as well as the art of recitation. The Royal School of Dramatic Art, founded in 1680, was the first official training school for actors in France.

In the 19th century, training schools became more specialized, with training programs for theatre, film, and television actors. The most famous training schools were The Actor's Studio in New York, which was founded on Stanislavski's techniques, and the National Conservatory of Dramatic Art in Paris, which was the reference for French actors.

In the 20th century, new training schools were created to meet the needs of actors in a rapidly changing world. The Jacques Lecoq School in France, founded in the 1950s, developed a physical and gestural approach to actor training. Yale School of Drama in the United States, founded in 1924, created a curriculum for actors, directors, and playwrights.

There have been numerous and varied great actors throughout the history of theatre, each with their own style and technique. Some of the most famous actors are Laurence Olivier, Marlon Brando, Sarah Bernhardt, Ellen Terry, John Gielgud, Laurette Taylor, Eleonora Duse, Richard Burbage, and many more.

Lighting and Music

Lighting and music are two essential elements of theatre that create an ambiance, atmosphere, and context for actors on stage. They have an impact on how the audience perceives the action unfolding on stage and are therefore key elements for the success of a theatrical performance.

Lighting is used to highlight certain aspects of the scene,

such as characters, objects, or locations, and to create contrasts or special effects. It can be used to draw the audience's attention to a specific part of the scene, create the illusion of night or day, or create a particular ambiance for a specific scene.

Music, on the other hand, is used to evoke emotions and feelings in the audience. It can be used to underscore the action taking place on stage, give depth to the characters, or add an additional dimension to the story. It can also be used to create a transition between two scenes or to enhance the overall ambiance of the play.

The use of lighting and music can vary depending on the genre of theatre. For example, classical theatre often uses subdued lighting and soft music to create a calm and poised ambiance, while absurd theatre may use flashing lights and discordant music to create a sense of anxiety in the audience.

It is important for lighting and music designers to work closely with directors and actors to ensure that the lighting and music are suited to the story and characters. This may involve rehearsals, adjustments, and last-minute changes to ensure that everything works properly on the day of the performance.

Evolution of the Audience and Theatres

Theatre has always been an art form that captivates people's imagination. From its origins in rituals and religious ceremonies to its modern forms, theatre has always aimed to engage spectators and provide them with an immersive and emotional experience.

Over the centuries, the theatre audience has evolved significantly. In primitive societies, spectators were often members of the community who attended performances as part of religious rituals. In ancient Greek theatre, spectators were mostly free men, although women also attended some performances. Spectators were often divided into sections based on their social rank and wealth. Roman spectators were more diverse, but the social elite often had reserved seats in the best locations.

In the Middle Ages, the audience often consisted of members of the working class and peasantry who attended shows for entertainment. During the Renaissance, the theatre audience expanded to include the aristocracy, merchants, and middle-class people. Theatre was often used as a means to assert social status and display wealth. Shows were also used to educate the audience about subjects such as morality and religion.

In the 17th century, the French theatre audience was very disciplined, with strict rules of behavior and etiquette. Theatre was often a place where people went to be seen and where they could assert their social status. In the 18th century, the audience became more diverse, with performances attracting a wide range of people. Playwrights also began to address more political and social issues.

In the 19th century, the theatre audience became even more diverse, with plays addressing more complex themes and nuanced characters. Spectators often came from all social classes, leading to an evolution of theatre towards more universal and accessible subjects. Theatres also evolved to meet these changes, with larger and more modern theatres.

In the 20th century, theatre continued to evolve to meet the needs of an increasingly diverse audience. Absurd and existentialist theatre attracted a younger and more avant-garde audience, while epic theatre and politically engaged theatre attracted a politically active audience. New forms of representation, such as immersive and interactive theatre, also attracted a younger and more experimental audience.

Today, the theatre audience is more diverse than ever, with spectators of all ages and social backgrounds. Theatre venues have also evolved to meet the needs of this audience, with more flexible and adaptable spaces that allow for a wide variety of productions and performance styles. Technological innovations have also allowed for new forms of theatre production, including multimedia projections, special effects, and high-quality sound equipment.

Critics and Awards

In the world of theatre, critics and awards have always been considered important elements for evaluating the quality of a production. Critics, often written by professionals in journalism and theatre criticism, are detailed evaluations of a play, performance, or production. They aim to inform the public, educate readers about forms and styles of theatre, guide audiences to productions that may interest them, and help artists refine their craft.

Critics can be positive, negative, or neutral, and critics' opinions can vary greatly depending on their experience, education, culture, and personal preferences. However, critics are often regarded as an important gauge for measuring the success of a production. They can help improve the quality of future productions, guide the public to quality productions, and help artists better understand their craft.

Awards, on the other hand, are honors conferred by professional organizations to reward excellence in different categories, such as best play, best actor, best actress, best director, etc. Awards can help draw attention to a particular production or artist, give well-deserved recognition to artists and producers, and stimulate creativity and innovation by encouraging artists to reach new heights.

The most prestigious awards in the theatre world include the Tony Awards on Broadway, the Laurence Olivier Awards in London, and the Molière Awards in France. These awards are often considered indicators of quality and prestige in the theatre industry. However, there are many other awards given worldwide, as well as theatre festivals and competitions that provide artists with opportunities to gain recognition.

While critics and awards are important in the theatre world, it is also important to remember that the appreciation of art is subjective and not everyone will appreciate the same productions in the same way. Critics and awards should therefore not be considered definitive judgments but rather opinions among others.

Furthermore, awards do not necessarily guarantee the

commercial success of a production or the satisfaction of the audience. Some critically acclaimed productions have experienced commercial failure, while other popular productions have been ignored or criticized. Artistic quality and audience satisfaction are complex elements that cannot be simply measured by critics and awards.

Theatre Around the World

Chinese Theatre

Chinese theatre is an incredibly rich and diverse form of performing art with a long and fascinating history dating back over two thousand years. It is characterized by a unique blend of ancient and modern traditions, as well as its great cultural and social importance in China.

The roots of Chinese theatre can be traced back to the Zhou dynasty over 2,000 years ago, where religious ceremonies included dramatic performances. Over the following dynasties, theatrical performances evolved to include a wide variety of opera forms, historical plays, tragedies, comedies, and musical dramas.

Traditional Chinese theatre is often associated with Chinese opera, which combines singing, dancing, acrobatics, and acting. The costumes are often sumptuous and the set designs elaborate. The stories are often based on Chinese mythology, classical literature, or Chinese history, with characters often being archetypes such as warriors, princesses, gods, and demons.

The acting style in Chinese theatre is often based on an aesthetic of exaggeration, with stylized movements and gestures. Actors often undergo years of training from a young age to learn the necessary techniques of singing, dancing, and acting to become professional actors. They are also trained in the mastery of traditional Chinese musical instruments.

In addition to Chinese opera, there are a wide variety of other forms of Chinese theatre, including puppet theatre, shadow theatre, lion dance theatre, and dragon dance theatre. Each of these forms has its own unique acting styles, costumes, and set designs.

Over time, Chinese theatre has undergone modernization with the emergence of contemporary theatre. Contemporary theatre often themes on social and political issues, minimalist aesthetics, and a more naturalistic acting style. This evolution has been influenced by European artistic movements of the 20th century, as well as other forms of Asian performing arts such as Japanese theatre and Indonesian puppet theatre.

Furthermore, Chinese theatre has also influenced performing arts worldwide, most notably Beijing opera, which was introduced to Europe in the early 20th century and influenced artists such as Maurice Ravel and Claude Debussy.

Japanese Theatre

Japanese theatre, also known as Noh, is a traditional form of stage art that dates back to the 14th century. Noh is characterized by highly stylized performances, beautifully ornate costumes, and complex masks. It is considered one of the oldest forms of theatre still actively performed in the world and remains a culturally significant component of Japanese society.

Noh is often regarded as a sacred art, as its roots lie in Shinto and Buddhist religious rituals. Noh plays are often based on stories from Japanese mythology and classical literature, with themes often revolving around spirituality, life, death, reincarnation, and the nature of existence. Characters often represent historical figures, ghosts, or deities.

Noh performances are typically carried out by a small number of actors, accompanied by a chorus and musicians playing traditional instruments such as drums and flutes. The actors' movements are slow and controlled, and the plays are often performed on a small wooden stage called a butai. The butai is designed to represent a shrine or temple, and the sets are often minimalist.

One of the most distinctive features of Noh is the use of masks, which are often made from cedar wood and hand-painted. Masks are used to represent different characters, such as deities, ghosts, and historical figures. Masks allow actors to express emotions and communicate information to the audience without relying on facial expressions.

Noh has had a significant influence on other art forms in Japan, including Kabuki and Bunraku. Kabuki, which is more popular theatre, is more dynamic and utilizes more elaborate costumes and sets. Bunraku is a puppet theatre that employs life-sized puppets to represent characters.

Though Noh is an ancient art form, it continues to be practiced and appreciated in Japan today. Noh performances are often organized during traditional festivals and religious celebrations, as well as in specialized theatres in major cities throughout Japan. Noh artists are considered guardians of this important cultural tradition, and new generations continue to be trained in specialized schools to preserve this unique form of stage art.

Indian Theatre

Indian theatre is one of the oldest and richest forms of theatre in the world. It has developed from religious rituals and is closely tied to Indian culture and spirituality. The early forms of theatre in India were often presented during religious ceremonies and served to impart moral teachings to members of the community. Over time, Indian theatre evolved to include secular stories and social themes.

Indian theatre can be divided into several categories based on region, language, and style. Each of these forms of theatre has its own unique characteristics, but all are imbued with the rich culture and spirituality of India.

One of the most well-known forms of theatre in India is shadow theatre, or Rangoli. This form of theatre uses shadow puppets to tell stories. The puppets are cut out of rice paper or buffalo hide and lit by oil lamps. Shadow theatre is often used to tell mythological and religious stories. This form of theatre originated in southern India and is very popular in the states of Tamil Nadu, Andhra Pradesh, and Karnataka.

Another popular form of theatre in India is Yakshagana, which originated in the state of Karnataka. This form of theatre is a combination of music, dance, and drama. Actors wear colorful costumes and elaborate makeup to portray mythological or historical characters. Yakshagana is often accompanied by live music played on traditional Indian instruments such as flute, drum, and violin.

Kathakali is another popular form of theatre in India. Originating in the state of Kerala, Kathakali combines dance and drama. Actors wear elaborate costumes and makeup to portray mythological or historical characters. Kathakali is often accompanied by live music played on traditional Indian instruments such as mridangam and chenda.

Nautanki is a popular form of theatre in northern India. This form of theatre uses songs and dance to tell stories. Actors wear colorful costumes and elaborate makeup. Nautanki is often used to tell love stories or social stories.

Additionally, Indian theatre has also undergone a modern revolution through playwrights such as Rabindranath Tagore and Girish Karnad. Their plays deal with social and political themes and have had a significant impact on Indian society. Tagore's plays have also been adapted for film and television. Contemporary playwrights continue to explore new themes and use modern techniques to tell their stories.

African Theatre

African theatre is a highly diverse and traditional art form. The forms and styles vary depending on the region, culture, and history of each country. African Theatre is often associated with rituals and community celebrations, as well as the transmission of knowledge and cultural values. However, it expands beyond these practices and is capable of exploring contemporary issues while drawing from its rich history.

African theatre is characterized by the use of music, dance, and spoken word to tell stories. Performances are often interactive, involving audience participation and creating a festive and communal environment. Costumes and masks are often used to symbolize characters and spirits, as well as to emphasize the importance of ritual and tradition. In some cultures, actors are considered messengers and healers, entrusted to convey spiritual messages and heal community ailments.

The origins of African theatre can be traced back to ancient times when theatrical forms were used in religious celebrations and rituals. Over time, these forms developed to include elements of everyday life and historical events, as well as Western and colonial influences. African theatre has also been influenced by Western dance, music, and literature, resulting in new artistic forms.

Modern African theatre often explores contemporary themes and issues such as corruption, war, migration, and human rights. Performances often reflect the tensions and challenges facing African societies while celebrating the richness and diversity of African culture. Theatre plays can question cultural and social norms while reflecting the traditions and values of the community.

Among the most well-known forms of African theatre are

West African masquerade theatre, East African puppet theatre, Central African oral theatre, and Southern African dance theatre. Each form has its own aesthetic, history, and cultural significance. For example, West African masquerade theatre uses masks to represent spirits and ancestors, while Central African oral theatre focuses on the use of speech and gestures to convey messages.

African theatre has also produced many notable artists and playwrights, such as Wole Soyinka, Athol Fugard, and Chinua Achebe, who have used theatre to explore social and political issues of their time. Their plays have been successful not only in Africa but also worldwide, contributing to the place of African theatre in the history of world theatre.

Finally, African theatre continues to evolve to meet the challenges of the 21st century. African artists explore new forms of theatrical expression, such as immersive and interactive theatre, while retaining the traditions and cultural values of their community. Increasingly, women and young artists are also contributing to the development of African theatre, thereby ensuring its vitality and relevance in modern society.

Latin American Theatre

Latin American theatre is a rich and diverse tradition that has developed in various countries across Latin America. This art form emerged within the context of Spanish and Portuguese colonization in the region but has been influenced by the Indigenous and African cultures present in Latin America.

Latin American theatre stands out by addressing important social, historical, and political themes for the region.

Latin American plays often explore issues related to injustice, poverty, discrimination, oppression, immigration, exile, and war. Latin American theatre has also been a tool for expressing the political and social commitment of many artists, especially in the 1960s and 1970s. During that time, theatre was used as a means of protesting against the military dictatorships in some Latin American countries.

The most well-known Latin American playwrights are famous writers such as Gabriel Garcia Marquez, Mario Vargas Llosa, and Pablo Neruda. Their plays have been adapted for the stage and performed worldwide. However, there are also many other talented but lesser-known playwrights who are immensely important to their countries and cultures. Among them are Griselda Gambaro (Argentina), Luis Rafael Sánchez (Puerto Rico), Augusto Boal (Brazil), and Osvaldo Dragún (Argentina).

Latin American theatre is characterized by its particular aesthetic, which often includes minimalist sets that highlight the performances of actors and the story being told. Music is also an important element in most Latin American theater productions, reflecting the Indigenous and African influences in the region. Latin American theatre productions are often created with modest means and limited budgets, yet they remain creative and captivating.

Some of the most famous theaters in Latin America can be found in Brazil, Argentina, Colombia, and Mexico. These theaters have played important roles in the development of Latin American theatre by providing platforms for local playwrights and actors. For example, the Teatro Municipal de São Paulo (Brazil), one of the largest theaters in Latin America, was founded in 1911 and has hosted globally renowned theatre, opera, and dance productions.

Latin American theatre has also been influenced by European artistic movements such as surrealism, existentialism, and theatre of the absurd. This has led to the emergence of new forms of theatre in Latin America, such as Theatre of the Oppressed developed by Augusto Boal, which aimed to create plays that offer concrete solutions to social and political problems. Theatre of the Oppressed involves the audience in the process of theatrical creation, encouraging interaction and audience participation.

Furthermore, Latin American theatre has also been marked by the use of puppetry and pantomime. In Mexico, for example, the puppet tradition is very present in children's theatre. In Argentina, mime was popularized by the theatre company El Taller de los Guasos, which created experimental theatre productions using mime, clowning, and dance techniques.

Finally, Latin American theatre has also experienced specific national theatrical movements in each country. For example, Chilean theatre was influenced by socialist and Marxist movements, whereas Brazilian theatre was influenced by the tropicalist movement of the 1960s, which blended popular music, theatre, and visual art.

Overall, Latin American theatre continues to evolve and remain a vibrant and important expression of the region's culture and history. It continues to explore new themes, techniques, and social issues, ensuring its continued relevance in contemporary society.

Theatre Professions

Actors and Actresses

Actors and actresses are essential craftsmen of the theatre, those who embody the characters and bring the story to life. Their role is crucial for the success of a theatrical production, as they are responsible for conveying the emotions, feelings, and ideas of the dramatic text to the audience.

Actors and actresses are versatile artists, capable of adapting to different roles and working in various contexts, from classical theatre to contemporary theatre, and across diverse genres. They must be able to master a wide range of acting techniques, interpretation, voice, movement, and psychology, as well as portraying different characters with accuracy and credibility.

The art of interpretation also requires actors and actresses to possess great sensitivity, deep understanding of human psychology, and the ability to connect with the audience by creating a strong emotional relationship. To succeed in this field, actors and actresses must be willing to work hard, constantly train, experiment, and take risks.

However, being an actor is not easy and comes with challenges and obstacles. Actors and actresses are often faced with fierce competition, pressure to secure roles, and the need to manage their time and energy to meet the demands of the profession. They must also be able to handle criticism, rejection, and failures while staying motivated and passionate about their craft.

Moreover, the history of theatre shows that actors and actresses have often faced additional challenges due to their gender, race, sexual orientation, or gender identity. Despite this, many artists have managed to break barriers and become icons of theatre, leaving their mark on the history of this art form.

The work of an actor also involves close collaboration with other members of the theatre company. Actors and actresses work closely with directors, set designers, costume designers, lighting technicians, and technicians to create an immersive and unforgettable theatrical experience for the audience.

Finally, it is important to emphasize that actors and actresses are not just artists but also human beings with interests, passions, opinions, and aspirations outside of the theatre. They can also use their profession to convey messages or raise awareness about causes they care about.

Directors

Directors are key craftsmen of the theatre, as they are responsible for creating the overall vision of the production and staging the story being told. They are, in a way, the conductors of the show, coordinating all elements to create a coherent and captivating theatrical experience.

The director's role is to translate the author's intentions into a cohesive and meaningful artistic vision. To do this, they must possess a solid knowledge of history and theatrical styles, as well as the ability to work collaboratively with actors, technicians, and other members of the production team.

The director must also have a deep understanding of the stage space and set design elements such as scenery, costumes, lighting, and sound. They must be able to create dynamic and coherent staging, using these elements to enhance the message and tone of the story being told.

The role of the director has evolved over time, transitioning from being a mere coordinator to a full-fledged artistic creator. During the 20th century, directors began experimenting with new forms of theatrical expression, using techniques such as absurd theatre and engaged theatre to explore social and political issues.

Some directors have become famous for their unique style, innovative vision, and ability to push the boundaries of theatre. Names like Peter Brook, Robert Wilson, and Julie Taymor immediately come to mind.

Being a director is demanding and requires great dedication and passion for the theatrical art. Directors often work long hours and must be prepared to face creative, technical, and financial challenges. But for those who succeed, it is one of the most rewarding professions in the theatre industry.

instruments.

In addition to Chinese opera, there are a wide variety of other forms of Chinese theatre, including puppet theatre, shadow theatre, lion dance theatre, and dragon dance theatre. Each of these forms has its own unique acting styles, costumes, and set designs.

Over time, Chinese theatre has undergone modernization with the emergence of contemporary theatre. Contemporary theatre often themes on social and political issues, minimalist aesthetics, and a more naturalistic acting style. This evolution has been influenced by European artistic movements of the 20th century, as well as other forms of Asian performing arts such as Japanese theatre and Indonesian puppet theatre.

Furthermore, Chinese theatre has also influenced performing arts worldwide, most notably Beijing opera, which was introduced to Europe in the early 20th century and influenced artists such as Maurice Ravel and Claude Debussy.

Japanese Theatre

Japanese theatre, also known as Noh, is a traditional form of stage art that dates back to the 14th century. Noh is characterized by highly stylized performances, beautifully ornate costumes, and complex masks. It is considered one of the oldest forms of theatre still actively performed in the world and remains a culturally significant component of Japanese society.

Noh is often regarded as a sacred art, as its roots lie in Shinto and Buddhist religious rituals. Noh plays are often based on stories from Japanese mythology and classical literature, with themes often revolving around spirituality, life, death, reincarnation, and the nature of existence. Characters often represent historical figures, ghosts, or deities.

Noh performances are typically carried out by a small number of actors, accompanied by a chorus and musicians playing traditional instruments such as drums and flutes. The actors' movements are slow and controlled, and the plays are often performed on a small wooden stage called a butai. The butai is designed to represent a shrine or temple, and the sets are often minimalist.

One of the most distinctive features of Noh is the use of masks, which are often made from cedar wood and hand-painted. Masks are used to represent different characters, such as deities, ghosts, and historical figures. Masks allow actors to express emotions and communicate information to the audience without relying on facial expressions.

Noh has had a significant influence on other art forms in Japan, including Kabuki and Bunraku. Kabuki, which is more popular theatre, is more dynamic and utilizes more elaborate costumes and sets. Bunraku is a puppet theatre that employs life-sized puppets to represent characters.

Though Noh is an ancient art form, it continues to be practiced and appreciated in Japan today. Noh performances are often organized during traditional festivals and religious celebrations, as well as in specialized theatres in major cities

Playwrights and Screenwriters

Playwrights and screenwriters are artists who create the stories and dialogues that fuel theatre and cinema. Their contributions are essential in bringing characters and situations to life, moving and captivating the audience.

Over the centuries, many playwrights and screenwriters have left their mark on the worlds of theatre and cinema. In ancient Greece, Aeschylus, Sophocles, Euripides, and Aristophanes wrote plays that have stood the test of time and are still performed today. In the Middle Ages, playwrights created religious plays that were used to educate the masses. During the Renaissance, William Shakespeare wrote plays that have become classics of English literature.

In the 17th century, French playwrights Corneille, Molière, and Racine created tragedies and comedies that elevated the theatrical genre to new heights. In the 18th century, Marivaux, Beaumarchais, and Voltaire introduced bourgeois drama and comedies of manners.

In the 19th century, romanticism led to the emergence of romantic drama, with authors such as Victor Hugo and Alexandre Dumas creating epic and dramatic works. Realism and naturalism also emerged, with playwrights such as Henrik Ibsen and Anton Chekhov exploring social and political issues of their time.

In the 20th century, the theatre of the absurd and existentialism were introduced by authors like Samuel Beckett, Eugène Ionesco, and Jean Genet, who experimented with different forms and styles. Epic theatre and theatre of engagement also emerged, with playwrights such as Bertolt Brecht, Jean-Paul Sartre, and Peter Weiss.

In the world of cinema, screenwriters have also played a key role. In the early 20th century, cinema pioneers such as Georges Méliès created fantastic stories that captivated audiences. Over time, screenwriters like Charlie Chaplin, Billy Wilder, and Woody Allen introduced comedies and dramas that redefined the genre.

Today, screenwriters like Quentin Tarantino, Aaron Sorkin, and Shonda Rhimes have created stories that have pushed the boundaries of the film and television industries. Their contributions have helped shape popular culture and have inspired many artists to follow in their footsteps.

Technicians and Designers

Technicians and designers are essential theatre professionals in the creation of successful theatrical productions. They often work behind the scenes, but their work is crucial in ensuring the success of each performance. Technicians are responsible for the creation and management of the technical aspects of the production, such as lighting, sound, video, special effects, scenery, costumes, and props. Designers, on the other hand, are visual artists who create plans, drawings, and models that guide the work of technicians and actors.

One of the first aspects to consider in the creation of a theatrical production is set design, i.e., the arrangement of the stage space. Technicians and designers work closely with directors and actors to create the appropriate atmosphere and environment for each play. They may be tasked with designing and constructing sets, costumes, props, and lighting according to the style and vision of the production.

Set design is a complex process that often involves teams of technicians and designers. The work may include designing plans, choosing materials, and constructing and installing sets. Technicians may also work on special effects, such as video projections, smoke machines, and special lighting, to add an extra dimension to the production.

Costumes and props are also important for creating a successful theatrical production. Costume designers work with actors to create outfits that reflect the era, style, and character of the characters. Props, such as furniture, weapons, books, and decorative objects, are often handcrafted to perfectly fit the production's universe.

Creating the sound ambiance is also important in staging a play. Sound technicians are responsible for the design, installation, and manipulation of audio systems used for dialogue, music, and sound effects. They may also work on creating musical compositions and soundtracks for the production.

Finally, lighting is also a crucial aspect of theatrical production. Lighting technicians work closely with designers to create visual effects that enhance the atmosphere of each scene. They may use lamps and spotlights to create shadows, silhouettes, and highlighting that accentuate the actors and sets.

Costumers and Makeup Artists

Costumers and makeup artists play a crucial role in the theatre. They are responsible for creating and bringing characters to life through their visual appearance. Costumes and makeups must be in line with the era and context of the show, as well as the personalities and characteristics of the characters.

Costumers are in charge of creating costumes that meet the production's needs, taking into account the allocated budget, historical periods, and cultures. They work closely with directors and actors to ensure that the costumes reflect the characters and the story of the play. Their work involves research, design, fabrication, and coordination with the rest of the technical team.

Makeup artists, on the other hand, are tasked with creating looks for the characters that align with their characteristics, ages, and personalities. Their work involves using professional makeup techniques to create special effects and transformations, such as scars, wounds, wrinkles, tattoos, etc. They also collaborate closely with costumers and directors to ensure that the costumes and makeup of the characters work together to create a complete image.

Costumers and makeup artists must be talented and creative artists, able to understand the needs and requirements of the production. They must also be able to work under pressure, meet deadlines, and manage their time and budget effectively.

The evolution of costumes and makeup over time is also an important aspect of theatre. Costumes and makeup can reflect different eras and cultures and can also be used to represent symbols or allegories. For example, clown makeup has become a universally recognized symbol for representing sadness and melancholy.

Ultimately, costumers and makeup artists can have an impact on the reception of the production. Poor costume or makeup choices can alter the audience's appreciation and comprehension of the story. Therefore, costumers and makeup artists must work diligently to ensure that their creations perfectly reflect the spirit of the play.

Stage Spaces and Scenography

The Evolution of Stage Spaces

The evolution of stage spaces is a key element in the history of theater. Since the origins of the discipline, performance venues have evolved to meet the needs of artists and audiences. Architecture and scenography have been influenced by the cultural, social, and economic trends of each era.

The earliest forms of theater were often ritual performances held in sacred spaces, such as temples or altars. With the rise of Greek civilization, theaters became permanent structures, built outdoors on hillsides to take advantage of the view. Greek theaters had a semi-circular shape and a stage device called a «skene,» which was used for costume and set changes.

During the Middle Ages, performance spaces were often churches or public squares. Actors would move around and the sets were minimal. During the Renaissance, theaters began to adopt more elaborate designs, influenced by classical Roman architecture and artistic trends of the time. The theaters of this period were characterized by a proscenium stage, with an arched opening for a clear view of the stage.

In the 17th century, French classical theater saw the emergence of Italian-style theaters, which featured a raised stage, an orchestra pit, and luxurious boxes for the audience.

Spanish Baroque theaters, on the other hand, were often circular in shape, with a central stage and a sophisticated system of pulleys for set changes.

In the 19th century, theaters developed into large spaces, such as English-style theaters, which featured balconies and tiers, as well as vast and elaborate stages. With the rise of the realist movement, stage sets began to imitate reality, leading to an increase in the size and complexity of sets.

In the 20th century, the evolution of stage spaces accelerated with the introduction of new technologies and artistic experimentation. The theaters of the absurd and the theater of engagement introduced new concepts of scenography, such as non-linear spaces and abstract sets. The theater of the oppressed also saw the introduction of new stage devices, such as theater forums.

Today, stage spaces continue to evolve with the adoption of digital technologies and other technical innovations. Productions can now be presented in immersive spaces, such as contemporary art installations or virtual reality environments. Traditional theaters have also adapted their stage spaces to offer a more immersive experience to the audience, using LED screens, video projections, and special effects to create unique visual worlds.

Elements of Scenography

Scenography is the art of creating the stage space, the space in which actors perform during a theatrical production. It encompasses all visual elements that contribute to creating the atmosphere and conveying the message of the play.

One of the most important elements of scenography is the set design, which can be realistic or stylized. The set design should be in harmony with the plot and characters, while also reflecting the time and place in which the action takes place. Decorative objects such as furniture, props, and costumes should also be consistent with the world of the play.

Lighting is another important element of scenography. It can be used to create different moods, highlight specific elements of the set or characters, or emphasize key moments in the plot. Lighting effects can be subtle or spectacular, depending on the needs of the play.

Music and sound effects are also key elements of scenography. They can contribute to creating a particular atmosphere, add depth to the characters' emotions, or highlight key moments in the plot. The music and sound effects should be in harmony with the theme of the play and the era in which it takes place.

Props are also important in creating the scenography. They can be used to create a particular atmosphere or highlight aspects of the characters. Props should be carefully selected to avoid distracting the audience or taking up too much space on stage.

Lastly, staging plays a crucial role in scenography. It should be in harmony with all other visual elements of the play and contribute to creating the overall atmosphere. Staging should also take into account the actors' movements on stage and the pace of the play.

Technological Innovations

In the field of theater, technological innovations have brought significant changes both in terms of production and the presentation of works. New technologies have allowed for the development of innovative theatrical forms, pushing the boundaries of imagination, making performances more immersive, and facilitating the creation of sets and special effects.

Theater began integrating technology as early as the early 20th century with the advent of electric lights and sound amplification. This made performances more visually striking and expanded creative possibilities. Nowadays, the latest technological innovations have opened up new possibilities, particularly with the arrival of digital technologies.

Video projections are among the most recent innovations in theater. Set designers can use large screens to project images that can instantly change, allowing for more complex and impressive sets. Projections can also be used to create special effects, animate sets, or create a particular ambiance.

Interactive theater is also becoming a reality thanks to the use of sensors and other technologies that allow the audience to actively participate in the play. Shows can be designed to be different every night, based on audience reactions.

Virtual reality is another technological innovation that is starting to be integrated into the world of theater. Audience members can wear virtual reality headsets to be transported into virtual worlds and participate in more immersive stories. This technology also makes it easier and more cost-effective to create virtual sets.

Lastly, the use of technology in actor training is a rapidly expanding field. Actors can use scene simulators to rehearse and prepare before performances. Technicians can also use augmented reality tools to visualize scenes before they are created.

Famous Theaters Around the World

Famous theaters around the world are witnesses to the history and culture of their respective countries. Each of these theaters is unique, with its own architectural style and atmosphere. Great theaters are gathering places for theater enthusiasts and artists from around the world, offering world-class performances and unforgettable experiences. Here are some of the most famous theaters around the world.

The Globe Theatre in London is one of the most famous theaters in the world, especially for Shakespeare enthusiasts. The original Globe Theatre was built in 1599 and was reconstructed in 1997 on its original site on the banks of the Thames. The reconstruction was done using traditional construction methods and period materials, providing an authentic experience for visitors. The shows presented at the Globe include productions of Shakespeare's works as well as plays by other classical authors.

The Bolshoi Theatre in Moscow is one of the most renowned theaters in the world for ballet and opera. The theater was built in 1825 and is considered one of the most beautiful theaters in the world. The Bolshoi is particularly known for its productions of classical ballet, including Swan Lake and The Nutcracker. The theater also has a large stage for operas and symphony concerts.

The Sydney Opera House in Australia is an architectural masterpiece famous worldwide for its distinctive shell-shaped design. The building was designed by Danish architect Jørn Utzon and was inaugurated in 1973. The Sydney Opera House is a true Australian icon, attracting visitors from around the world to attend operas, ballets, and classical music concerts.

Carnegie Hall in New York is a historic theater famous for its acoustic quality. It was opened in 1891 and is considered one of the best concert venues in the world. Carnegie Hall has hosted many great artists and musicians, including Leonard Bernstein, Duke Ellington, Benny Goodman, Judy Garland, and the Beatles. The theater is also famous for its concert organ, which is one of the largest and most famous in the world.

The National Theatre of Chaillot in Paris is a famous theater known for its diverse programming of dance, theater, circus, and music performances. The theater was built for the 1937 Paris Universal Exposition and was restored in 2006. The National Theatre of Chaillot is also famous for its breathtaking view of the Eiffel Tower, providing a spectacular backdrop for performances.

These few examples of famous theaters around the world represent just a small fraction of the cultural richness offered by theaters worldwide. Theater lovers can also discover other renowned theaters such as the Teatro Colón in Buenos Aires, the Vienna State Opera, the Mariinsky Theatre in St. Petersburg, the Royal Theatre of La Monnaie in Brussels, the Royal Albert Hall in London, and many more.

Each of these famous theaters offers a unique and unforgettable experience for theater enthusiasts, providing a glimpse into the history, culture, and traditions of the countries in which they are located. Visitors can enjoy not only the performances presented but also the architecture, decor, and special atmosphere of each theater.

Theatre and Other Arts

Music and Opera

Music and opera are two key elements in the art of the stage and have played a crucial role in the history of theatre. Music, in particular, is an essential tool for creating atmosphere and conveying emotions. In the context of theatre, it can be used to enhance the drama and emotion of the actors or to underscore key moments in the action. Opera, on the other hand, is a form of theatrical art in which the action is told through song and musical dialogue.

The origins of opera date back to the 16th century in Italy, where composers such as Claudio Monteverdi began integrating musical elements into theatrical plays. Over the centuries, opera has evolved to include varied musical styles, from recitatives to arias, ensembles, and choruses. Operas can be classified based on musical style, plot, production, and place of origin.

Furthermore, music is often used in other forms of theatre, such as musicals, where music is used to tell the story and characters sing and dance on stage. Musicals are often considered a distinct genre from musical theatre, which focuses more on music and dance than on plot.

It is also worth noting that music and opera have often been used to disseminate political and social messages. Operas can contain hidden political messages, and music can be used to create a sense of patriotism or protest. For example,

Verdi's operas have been used as symbols of Italian unity, while Richard Wagner's German opera was associated with the rise of German nationalism in the 19th century.

In summary, music and opera are important elements of theatre that have played a crucial role in its history. They have been used to enhance emotions and dramatic effect, as well as to convey political and social messages. Opera, in particular, has evolved to include different musical styles and is a distinct art form that remains popular today.

Dance and Ballet

Dance and ballet are forms of performance art that have a long history and significant influence on theatre. Ballet is a form of classical dance characterized by pointe technique, foot positions, and graceful movements. It originated in Italy in the 15th century, but it was in France that ballet saw its most significant development.

In the 17th century, King Louis XIV of France was a great ballet enthusiast and played a significant role in its development. He founded the Royal Academy of Dance in 1661 to formalize classical dance technique and even danced in many ballets himself. Early ballets were court entertainments, featuring sumptuous costumes and elaborate sets. However, with the arrival of Romantic ballet in the 19th century, ballet became a more emotional and dramatic art form.

With the establishment of professional ballet companies

such as the Paris Opera Ballet, the Royal Danish Ballet, and the Royal Ballet in London, ballet became a respected performance art and gained popularity worldwide.

Contemporary dance, on the other hand, is a more free and expressive form of dance that developed in the late 1800s and early 20th century. It was influenced by choreographers such as Martha Graham, Isadora Duncan, and Merce Cunningham, who rejected the conventions of classical ballet and sought to create a more personal and expressive dance form.

In recent decades, contemporary dance has become more diverse, incorporating elements from different dance styles, as well as unconventional movement and expression forms.

Dance and ballet continue to play an important role in theatre and culture in general. They can be used to express emotions, tell stories, and create captivating visual and auditory experiences for the audience. They are also a means for dancers to express themselves and connect with their audience in a very personal way.

Cinema and Visual Arts

Cinema and visual arts have had a significant influence on the evolution of theatre throughout its history. Indeed, these arts have brought new ideas in terms of storytelling, staging, and the use of stage space.

When cinema was born in the late 19th century, it quickly

influenced theatre by introducing new techniques such as editing, more naturalistic acting, and the projection of images in the background. This influence was particularly strong in the 1920s with the avant-garde theatre movement, which sought to integrate cinematic techniques into theatrical productions.

In the 1960s, performances by the Judson Dance Theater also had an impact on theatre by introducing movement and choreography elements into theatrical productions. These performances often emphasized the interaction between artists and stage space, which influenced how set and lighting designers approach scenography.

Moreover, cinema and visual arts have also influenced theatre in the way stories are told. Theatrical productions have borrowed elements from cinematic storytelling, such as flashbacks, cutscenes, and smooth transitions, to create a more seamless experience for the audience.

However, while these arts have brought new ideas and techniques, they have also been criticized for their ability to overshadow the unique qualities of theatre as an autonomous art form. Indeed, some critics argue that excessive use of visual elements in theatrical productions can detract from the expressive power of live performance.

Despite this, cinema and visual arts continue to influence contemporary theatre. Video projections, special effects, scenographic techniques, and choreography have been successfully integrated into many contemporary theatrical productions.

Theatre and Society

Theatre as a Tool of Power and Propaganda

Theatre has always been a powerful communication tool, capable of conveying messages and ideas in a persuasive manner. As such, it has often been used as a tool of power and propaganda by governments, political parties, and religious organizations to influence public opinion and justify their actions.

The history of theatre is full of examples of plays that were created with the specific purpose of manipulation or persuasion. In the Middle Ages, for example, mysteries and moralities were used to teach the principles of the Catholic religion and convince people of the superiority of the Church. In the 17th century, French classical theatre was used to promote the values of absolute monarchy and criticize political opponents.

In the 20th century, theatre was used as a propaganda tool in totalitarian regimes such as Nazi Germany and the Soviet Union. Bertolt Brecht's plays in East Germany were created with the aim of promoting communist ideals and criticizing capitalist systems. Similarly, Soviet propaganda theatre was used to promote the communist regime and justify its actions to the population.

Theatre has also been used to influence public opinion in times of war. During World War I, British plays were created to encourage recruitment and support the war effort. During

World War II, plays were used to strengthen moral resistance and encourage solidarity.

However, theatre has not always been used in a negative way to influence public opinion. Many plays have been created to denounce social and political injustices and encourage awareness and action. Bertolt Brecht's plays, for example, were created with the aim of denouncing social inequalities and promoting revolution. Augusto Boal's plays were created to encourage active spectator participation in the theatrical process and promote social action.

Ultimately, theatre is a very powerful communication tool that can be used positively or negatively to influence public opinion. It is important to understand how it can be used for manipulation and persuasion in order to be aware of its potential effects. Theatre should be used responsibly to encourage reflection, awareness, and action.

Theatre and Social and Political Issues

Theatre has always been closely linked to the social and political issues of its time. From its origins in religious rituals and tribal ceremonies to contemporary forms of performance, theatre has been a means of commenting on, critiquing, and questioning the ideas and practices that govern life in society.

Throughout history, theatre has often been used as a tool of power and propaganda by authoritarian regimes and incumbent governments. Plays were often censored and controlled by authorities to avoid any criticism or questioning of the status quo.

However, theatre has also been a means for artists to oppose authoritarian regimes and advocate for human rights. Plays have been created to raise awareness among the masses about social and political issues and promote ideas of justice and equality.

In the Middle Ages, theatre was often used to portray religious life and teach the principles of the Christian faith. Plays were performed in public squares, and actors often traveled from town to town to spread their message. Mysteries, miracles, and moralities were the earliest forms of medieval theatre.

During the Renaissance, theatre became a means for artists to reflect on humanity and its relationship with the world. William Shakespeare's plays explored universal themes such as love, betrayal, politics, and human nature. Theatre was also a means for artists to critique the society of their time. Molière's plays were used to ridicule the French aristocracy and its customs.

In the 18th century, theatre became a means for artists to critique the emerging bourgeois society. Bourgeois drama was a new genre of theatre that explored the social and political issues of the bourgeoisie. Plays by Marivaux and Beaumarchais were used to criticize social hierarchies and economic inequalities of their time.

In the 20th century, theatre became a means for artists to

question dominant ideas and practices in society. Absurdist and existentialist theatre explored questions of human existence and the human condition. Epic theatre and theatre of commitment were used to promote ideas of social justice and freedom.

Contemporary theatre has continued to be a means for artists to engage with the social and political issues of their time. Postmodern theatre has challenged ideas of reality and truth, while immersive and interactive theatre has reimagined the relationship between the audience and the artist.

The Role of Theatre in Education and Training

Theatre has always been considered an art form that plays an important role in education and training. It is a powerful means of conveying values, ideas, and emotions to a diverse audience. Studies have shown that theatre audiences tend to be more empathetic, creative, critical, and receptive to different ideas and perspectives. That is why theatre can be used in an educational context to help students develop their social and emotional skills, creativity, and critical thinking.

In formal education, theatre can be used to teach skills such as communication, public speaking, active listening, and problem-solving. For example, theatre exercises can help students improve their diction, posture, gestures, and ability to interact with others. Role-playing can also help students understand different points of view, step into the shoes of other characters, and resolve conflicts constructively.

Outside of formal education, theatre can also be used in an informal educational context. Theatre workshops for youth, for example, can help children develop their creativity, self-confidence, and self-esteem. Community theatres can also offer training programs for adults seeking to improve their communication and public speaking skills.

Theatre can also be used to address important social and political issues in an educational context. Plays that tackle subjects such as racism, discrimination, poverty, and violence can help students understand social issues and develop their critical awareness. Theatre workshops can also be used to encourage students to engage in social and political causes that matter to them.

Finally, theatre can also help students develop an appreciation for the arts and culture. Theatre performances can help students understand different forms of artistic expression and develop their aesthetic sensitivity. Theatre visits and field trips can also provide unique opportunities for students to discover new cultures and forms of artistic expression.

Theatre and Therapy: Theatre as a Tool for Personal Transformation

Theatre is an art form that has always had a significant impact on society and individuals. From its origins in primitive societies, theatre has been used to entertain, inform, inspire, and mobilize people. But it has also been used as a tool for personal transformation and healing.

Therapeutic theatre, also known as healing theatre, is a form of therapy that uses theatrical performance as a means of healing and personal development. This practice focuses on the emotional, cognitive, and social aspects of the individual and uses the power of creativity and expression to help people overcome their problems.

There are several forms of therapeutic theatre, including forum theatre, improvisational theatre, theatre of the oppressed, narrative theatre, and more. In each case, the aim is to enable participants to emotionally liberate themselves, gain a better understanding of their emotions and behavior, and develop social and communication skills.

Therapeutic theatre can be used to address a wide range of mental and physical health issues, such as depression, anxiety, eating disorders, trauma, personality disorders, addiction, and more. It can also help individuals improve their self-confidence, self-esteem, creativity, empathy, and problem-solving abilities.

Numerous studies have been conducted on the beneficial effects of therapeutic theatre. For example, one study showed that cancer patients who participated in theatre workshops reported a significant improvement in their quality of life and emotional well-being. Another study showed that improvisational theatre can help individuals with social anxiety disorders improve their self-confidence and ability to socially interact.

Therapeutic theatre is often used in conjunction with other forms of therapy, such as psychotherapy and medication therapy. It can be used in group or individual settings and is often facilitated by qualified mental health professionals, such as psychologists, social workers, counselors, art therapists, and more.

One of the reasons why therapeutic theatre is so effective is that it provides a safe and creative space for exploring emotions, thoughts, and behaviors. Participants are encouraged to express their feelings and thoughts in creative and imaginative ways, which can help release repressed emotions and understand negative thought patterns.

Additionally, therapeutic theatre can help develop social and communication skills, such as empathy, nonverbal communication, active listening, collaboration, and problem-solving. These skills are vital for improving relationships with others and navigating the world more effectively.

Another reason why therapeutic theatre is effective is that it uses storytelling to allow participants to tell their own stories. By telling their stories, participants can gain a better understanding of their own lives, identity, and place in the world. This understanding can help develop greater resilience and better cope with life's challenges.

Lastly, therapeutic theatre uses performance to allow participants to see themselves in a new light. By playing different roles, participants can experiment with new ways of being and thinking. This can help develop new skills and perspectives about oneself and others.

Therapeutic theatre can be used in various settings, such as schools, hospitals, prisons, community centers, mental health clinics, and more. It is often used to help individuals who have difficulty expressing their emotions or have experienced traumatic events.

Challenges and Perspectives of Theatre in the 21st Century

Economic Stakes and the Survival of Theatre Companies

Theatre is an art form with a long history and great significance in our society. However, it faces numerous economic challenges, particularly due to the high costs associated with producing a play. Actors' salaries, sets, costumes, and other expenses can quickly accumulate, and theatre companies must find ways to finance these costs, whether through government grants, donations, or sponsorship.

Furthermore, theatre must compete with other forms of entertainment to attract and retain its audience. Theatre companies must be creative and innovative in their approach to offer unique and engaging experiences. This can include innovative marketing initiatives, collaborations with artists from different fields, special events, and educational programs.

Social media and online streaming platforms have also changed the way people consume cultural content. Theatre companies must adapt to these new consumption modes by offering digital experiences that reflect the essence of live performances while meeting the needs of modern audiences.

Moreover, the COVID-19 pandemic has had a significant

impact on the theatre industry. Travel restrictions and venue closures have affected theatre companies' ability to generate revenue. Theatre companies have had to adapt by offering online productions, organizing outdoor events, and adopting strict safety measures to protect artists and audiences.

Despite these economic challenges, theatre continues to be an important cultural force. Theatre companies must be creative and innovative in their approach to production and promotion. This may include collaborations with local businesses, crowdfunding initiatives, and sponsorship programs for companies.

Theatre companies must also remain true to their artistic mission and continue to offer unique and engaging experiences for their audience. This can include innovative theatre productions and collaborations with artists from different backgrounds. Theatre companies can also offer educational programs to raise awareness about the importance of theatre art and encourage young artists to pursue a career in this field.

Ultimately, the survival and prosperity of theatre depend on theatre companies' ability to adapt to the economic realities of the industry while remaining true to their artistic vision. Theatre is a timeless art form that has the ability to deeply and meaningfully touch people, and it is important that we support and encourage its ongoing development.

Invitation to Reconnect with Theatre in the 21st Century

In today's world, theatre can sometimes seem like a forgotten art, drowned in a sea of digital entertainment and social media. Yet, the art of the stage is more alive than ever, offering a unique, immersive, and captivating experience that cannot be replicated by any other medium.

Indeed, theatre is an unparalleled human experience. As spectators, we sit in the same room as the actors, sharing their space and energy. We witness the creativity and ingenuity of live artists, with all the risks and surprises that entails. This creates a special connection between the audience and the actors, an emotional bond that cannot be matched by screens. Theatre offers us the opportunity to live a shared human experience, to witness the emotion, vulnerability, and humanity of the actors in real-time.

Moreover, theatre can be a powerful force for social and political change. Plays can explore complex issues in a deep and insightful manner, helping raise awareness and provoke reflection on subjects such as social justice, diversity, equality, and the environment. Theatre can give a voice to the marginalized and the excluded, providing a platform to tell their stories and share their experiences. It can thus encourage empathy and inclusion by showing us different perspectives and helping us understand the realities of others.

Finally, theatre is constantly evolving, with new genres, forms, and styles emerging all the time. New technologies, innovative stage design techniques, and bold staging concepts continually push the boundaries of what is possible on stage. Theatre is also becoming more inclusive, with initiatives to encourage diversity among artists and audiences, as well as to explore new forms of interactive participation. The possibilities are endless, ranging from immersive and interactive plays to outdoor performances to modern adaptations of classic plays.

Acknowledgment

Dear reader,

First and foremost, allow me to express how moved I am that you have made it to the end of this book. I know it is a considerable undertaking, and I truly appreciate your commitment to the subject of theatre history.

In writing this book, I aimed to share my passion for the art of the stage with you and give you a glimpse into the very essence of theatre. I hope that my fresh, innovative, and thought-provoking insights on the subject have successfully captivated and inspired you.

I would like to emphasize that this book would not have been possible without the help and support of numerous theatre professionals, researchers, and experts in the field. I would like to thank them wholeheartedly for their invaluable contributions.

Lastly, I would like to personally thank you for taking the time to read this book. I hope it has brought you joy and helped you better understand the importance and impact of theatre in our society.

With my sincerest regards,

Lionel.

Printed in Great Britain
by Amazon